Narcissistic Friend

How to Identify, Subdue, and
Safeguard Yourself from
Narcissistic Friends. Observe for
Behavior Signs, Sociopath
Tendencies, and Learn to
Recognize the Covert Narcissistic
Personality Disorder

Mona Diggins

advice. The content within this book has been derived from various sources. Please consult a licensed professional before attempting any techniques outlined in this book.

By reading this document, the reader agrees that under no circumstances is the author responsible for any losses, direct or indirect, that are incurred as a result of the use of the information contained within this document, including, but not limited to, errors, omissions, or inaccuracies.

Table of Contents

Introduction

"When someone treats you like crap, just remember it's because there's something wrong with them, not you. Normal people don't go around destroying other people's lives."

~ Anonymous

A smile that reveals kindness but holds a sinister intent. A hug that promises comfort but carries nefarious motivations. A love that feels genuine but clutches pernicious machinations.

Sound familiar? If any of the above statements do, then you should consider yourself fortunate. I know, you might be appalled that I would think of your situation as one residing in "good fortune." But what you have is an awareness that many do not possess. You have come to realize something quite disturbing. It's a truth that you had to accept despite playing around with it and hoping against hope that it might just be a lie.

Your friend is a narcissist.

That's a difficult statement to admit. It carries with it a certain weight and understanding. There is a realization embedded in the statement, one that says that things will never go back to the way they were.

That is okay. While it is a bitter pill to swallow, the fact that you have decided to accept your situation is the first and the biggest step toward change.

Or perhaps you might not be entirely sure what to make of your friend. You know that there is something amiss. It might have been quite difficult for you to grasp in the beginning, but over time, you realize that you cannot ignore it anymore. What you once considered 'normal' might start nagging at your mind. You feel like there is a flaw somewhere, but you are unable to put your finger on it. Eventually, you realize that the only choice left to you is one that involves action. You want to do something about it, but you have no idea what or where to start.

Whether you are aware of what is happening in your life or you have come here for answers, I bid you welcome. I want you to know that you are in a safe space. You are welcome here and no judgment is passed on your situation. You can be entirely honest knowing that within the following pages, you are going to receive acceptance. More importantly, you are going to discover help.

But before we delve into the thick of things, let's get to know each other. Allow me to introduce myself. I am Mona Diggins. Lover of classic rock and jazz. Admirer of Christopher Nolan's work (*Inception* is his best movie, prove me wrong). Cat lady (just one cat short of adding the 'crazy' prefix). Author (you make that possible by the way, and I want you to pat yourself on the back for that. In fact, we're going to perform a lot of 'back-patting' along the way. Trust me, you are going to need it). Athlete, and I also have a pretty strong badminton arm if I say so myself. I have traveled around the world but haven't managed to tick off all of the countries on my bucket list. And I am a foodie. Give me a plate of Thai red curry and it won't be difficult to see who is the most content person in the room.

Those are pretty good things to say about myself, right? I mean, I should be writing a book on positivity, not narcissism. You might imagine a white picket fence, a green and well-mowed lawn, porch chairs, exquisite dinner sets, and a brand-new SUV in the garage. Of course, there's me smack-dab in the middle of the house, a suburban mom getting her kids ready for school and enjoying an idle chat with her busy husband.

Allow me to paint another picture.

I suffered abuse from my partner.

Actually, let's take that canvas away for a little bit and look at an older painting.

I was 14 when I realized my best friend was a narcissist.

It didn't occur to me at the beginning. I loved her implicitly. After all, having best friends at that age feels like joining a Fortune 500 company; you feel like at least a part of your future is going to be okay. In this case, I believed that I had formed a bond that would last for a long time.

Oh, silly, silly hubris, how you strike at the core of foolishness to reveal the folly of human beings.

I cannot claim to have come across the realization that my friend was a narcissist on my own. It was—and here is the plot twist—my best friend's mother who confided her daughter's personality to me. Perhaps it was because of how much time I had spent at my friend's house. I had gotten to know her family, and they had welcomed me into their household as one of their own. Or maybe it was because her mother felt more comfortable talking to me, owing to long and wonderful conversations. Or perhaps the family had developed a sense of sympathy for me, knowing what their daughter was truly like, and was perhaps making me aware just enough to form my own opinions of her.

Regardless of the circumstances, my eyes were opened to narcissism for the first time. I realized how much effort and time I had put into my friendship and how I was the only one nurturing the relationship. I would listen to her problems, but she would barely provide even a modicum of attention for mine. I would be there for her, sometimes even in the middle of the night. Yet I was aware that she preferred to spend time with her own group of friends. There were so many things I ignored but finally admitted to myself after my talk with her mother.

From that moment on, I vowed to understand more about narcissism.

But then, love happened.

They say that love is blind. I say that it *makes* people blind.

I always assumed that there was just one kind of narcissist. It was only after I met my husband that I realized how narcissism can be such a clandestine trait. You think you might detect it early on, but too often, you are unable to sense its presence.

At this point, we add back the canvas we were working on; I suffered abuse from my husband.

And yet, here I am. Still married to him. I still love him in a way that does not mean I blindly accept anything he does. Before you assume that this is some twisted form of Stockholm Syndrome taking root in my psyche, I assure you it is not.

You see, I have grown to love myself more. I have two beautiful children who receive the best part of their parents' love. They don't see the true nature of their father, and for now, I would like to keep it that way. Of course, you might think my husband can't keep his narcissistic side hidden away for long, and I agree. Sometimes, I see it slipping through the cracks when he interacts with our children. However, the level of training he has done for himself is the result of a two-person job, his and mine.

The tale of my husband's redemption is a long one. However, knowing what he was capable of and suffering the abuse that he had inflicted on me changed my perspective. More importantly, it laid the foundation for a yearning to learn more about narcissism. This eventually led me on a quest to discover the true nature of this psychological condition and other personality disorders that, unfortunately, reside within the minds of people.

For the past five years, I have learned. I have studied extensively. I have attended lectures and met with professionals, including many who have published research on the subject. I have wanted to understand it on a level where I would be comfortable talking about it.

Because I realized something back when I was taking my first steps forward toward knowledge; I wanted to help others. I suppose I have always been that way. Just like the moments I had spent helping my "best friend" out of the scrapes she would find herself in without gaining even a sliver of respect or acknowledgment in return. However, helping other sufferers of narcissism feels different.

I know that people are taking the hits, bruises, and trauma in silence. I realize that many cannot find their voice or stand up for themselves. In many ways, I feel as though I share a connection with them, even though I may never meet them in person or otherwise. I suppose that this book is my conversation with them. It is my "hello," "you'll be okay," and "I'm here to help you" all rolled into one. Above everything, what I truly want to say is that you—whoever and wherever you are—can get through this. You don't have to be the victim all your life.

About a year and a half ago, I heard the sentence "Sweetheart, don't worry about the groceries. You take care of the kids while I get them."

I was stunned. It wasn't a statement I thought I would ever hear from my partner. I remember the look of confusion I threw at him, intermingled with my usual caution. After all, I was running through every conceivable idea that concluded that this was a scheme. It was a plan concocted by my husband to gain something from me. It was a nerve-wracking moment.

While my thoughts zipped around in my cranium, my husband stood there fidgeting with the hem of his shirt, a boyish awkwardness displayed on his face.

Then I realized something; for the first time since our marriage, I couldn't make myself believe that this man had ulterior motives even though I tried. I felt like a scientist. You see, in the world of science, the correct way to reach a certain conclusion is by looking at all of the contradictions first. If you have an answer for a contradiction, then you are that much closer to a convincing result. I realized that despite using every theory to convince myself of my husband's falsehood, they didn't work.

As he stood there, showing genuine kindness, I realized that I should not take this moment from him. I could have told him that it was alright and that I would go get the groceries. But I wanted him to go through the motions and fulfill his kindness. Only then would he feel like he earned it. And when one works to earn something, they cherish it immensely.

With a nod and a smile, I thanked him and told him to call me if there was something he wanted to clarify.

He beamed, eager to show this new side of himself, and quickly departed.

For the first time, I realized that all my efforts to make sure that I have control over my life, despite what my husband had done, had become reality. I know that you are going through your own challenges and tragedies with a narcissistic friend. In many ways, my husband was supposed to be my best friend. That never happened. Until recently when I decided to take my life into my hands.

That is what I want to offer you, the ability to grasp your life with your own rules. You can use the control you gain to decide what you want to do next. Would you like to maintain your friendship? Do you want to end your relationship for a fresh start? The choices are left to you. But the most important part is to give you those choices and the power to choose of your own volition.

It's time for you to become the person you always wanted to be.

There is one last point I want to draw your attention to. At the beginning of each chapter, I have added an affirmation. I am not going to ask you to consider these affirmations from a spiritual or psychological perspective. That is entirely up to you, and in whatever manner you would like to look at them, please feel free to do so. However, the most important idea is to truly understand the affirmation. I don't just mean its definition. I mean the way it relates to you. What does the statement mean to you? What kind of life does it conjure in your imagination? Think about them, and repeat them.

Because you deserve them.

Chapter 1:

Is Your Friend a Narcissist?

I am deserving of respect.

It's a unique word, respect. If I ask you to define it, you might provide bullet points to explain what you mean. But how can you truly explain what the word means? I am not talking about the dictionary definition. I'm sure the word's official meaning might make sense. In fact, you merely have to enter the word in Google, and you are presented with a meaningful definition.

My question is not in its description or comprehension since I'm sure we can comprehend the word if we set our minds to it. Rather, I want to talk about your interpretation of the word.

As children, we are given certain guidelines on respect. Make sure that you play nice. Apologize if you have made a mistake. Ask if you need something. Thank you. Have a nice day. You're welcome.

When you take the guidelines as a whole, you realize their value. We need to show kindness and common courtesy. If we are incapable of reaching out to our fellow human beings through positive influences, then how different are we from cavemen? In fact, take away the civility, respect, and love that we possess, then the only step toward living in a cave is to make grunting noises and wear loincloths.

It is when you take each guideline and analyze it that you can look at things from a different perspective. You see, it isn't just about saying "thank you." It is about knowing when to say it. And this goes for a lot of things whether you are apologizing, appreciating, or even complimenting. For example, you wouldn't necessarily walk up to a person and say, in the kindest way possible, "My, how ugly you look today." It doesn't show kindness at that point, does it?

Essentially, we are capable of respect and possess the understanding to show it in a way that matters.

There are two keywords, respect and understanding.

Why are those two words important? It is because narcissists can take the meaning of those words and twist them for nefarious purposes. Their "thank yous" are meant to hurt. In other words, they not only have a lack of respect for others but also a lack of understanding of how to show respect the right way. Or perhaps they know. Deep down, they know what they should be doing instead but choose not to. After all, admitting that they are wrong and that they need to do things differently is an unacceptable notion to them.

However, simply using the idea of respect as a yardstick to measure narcissism is folly and often perilous. When you label a person, that label sticks. Wrong labels lead to misunderstandings and unnecessary conflicts. More importantly, labels hurt. When you attach a word or phrase to a person, you give that person's entire character a meaning. If your definition of that person is wrong, then you are the cause of quite a bit of harm.

So, how can you identify if your friend is a narcissist?

A Friend Indeed?

I would like you to understand what I said about labels. They are powerful and capable of breaking down a person's character into smaller bits. Sometimes, those bits might look dangerous and threatening when they shouldn't be. For that reason, remember that everyone has a small degree of narcissism in them. If someone has one or even a couple of these traits, do not automatically place them into the narcissist category.

Exaggerated Sense of Self-Importance

Perhaps one of the defining traits of narcissists is that they have a gargantuan sense of self-importance. Narcissists are voracious eaters, and their foods are attention, praise, awe, and sometimes even reverence. They are mentally gluttonous, and their appetites cannot be satiated through a single portion. The only respect that they possess is for themselves. The respect that they show to others is, more often than not, manufactured.

A Belief That They Are Unique or Special

To them, their skills, experiences, knowledge, and ideas are badges of honor. Quite frankly, there isn't anything wrong with being proud of yourself, your accomplishments, or your ideas. Every now and then, you deserve to toot your own horn.

For narcissists, however, everything about them supersedes the accomplishments, traits, ideas, and knowledge of others. They are superior. Rather than improve themselves or learn, they choose to blow up their lack of knowledge and experience. It is also because of this that they look at people based on their achievements, not for who they are. They like to move around in circles where people have immense success, the flashiest possessions, extravagant lifestyles, or are simply useful to the narcissist.

Excessive Admiration

I have talked to many people who either live or are acquainted with narcissists. One of the most common symptoms I have noticed people complain about is that they are simply exhausted. A narcissist is a bottomless emotional well that needs constant refills. You need to supply them with praise and attention or they might react negatively. Your needs, on the other hand, are in the backseat. Actually, I would say that they are discarded in the trunk space, never to be considered again.

A Sense of Entitlement

Narcissists believe that they are deserving of something. What they deserve can either be something intangible, like attention, or tangible. For example, they could be in a restaurant and the waiter might be attending to someone else. To a narcissist, the waiter has to first reach out to them before anyone else. Failing to do so might convince the narcissist that the waiter has nothing but nefarious intentions, even though it might only be because the other patron had entered the restaurant earlier than the narcissist, and the waiter is merely doing their job. In such ways, if they are not served their demands for the day, they start displaying negative reactions, such as complaints, frustration, anger, disappointment, and in a few cases, even violence.

Empathy Is Minimal or Absent

Without empathy, people cannot form meaningful, emotional, and genuine bonds with others. The attachment a parent feels to a child, the love of a best friend, or the care displayed by a sibling are all possible because on some level, either consciously or unconsciously, people are capable of offering empathy. Narcissists are either incapable of showing empathy or they just don't care. When things are going their way, they can seem empathetic, even radiating warmth like their bodies are taken over by a different person. But as soon as things stop going their way, the facade drops. You are then privy to their true nature.

Envious of Others

Narcissists place themselves on a pedestal. They think that others are envious of them. However, what they are doing is projecting their envy onto someone else. In other words, they are the ones who are jealous of someone else, but they cannot accept that fact. In their denial, they convince themselves that others are jealous of them. Their envy isn't even the worst part. It is what they attempt to do to bring down a person they feel is superior at something. Name-calling, gossip, criticism, and downright abuse are just some of the weapons they hold in their offensive inventory.

Display Arrogance

Bear in mind that arrogance is present in everyone to a certain degree. Many people are just cocky, but that does not make them narcissists. So how can you distinguish between cockiness and narcissism? When someone is cocky, they tend to aggrandize their capabilities. They embellish their successes and overvalue their skills. They merely try to show off without intending to cause harm. Narcissists, on the other hand, have specific reasons for their arrogance. They want to cause damage to someone, or they simply want to make others feel bad. Their cockiness reaches an aggressive level where they want to attack someone or a group of people.

Delve Into the Fantastical

Narcissists love to create elaborate fantasies in their heads where they are the superior person. Their thoughts are spent on how they can easily find the perfect partner, or score a million dollars, or even find success. It is within these thoughts that they find comfort since their reality is something they do not want to accept. Narcissists sometimes don't like to put in the effort to accomplish something. They enjoy believing that things will just happen to them. This also ties in with their sense of entitlement. They don't want to take the difficult path toward a goal; they believe their goals will navigate the obstacles to reach them.

Taking Advantage of Others

We already established that narcissists tend to look at the accomplishments and usefulness of a person. There is a reason why. In their minds, they are already thinking about how they can take advantage of others. People might as well be the living equivalent of a spoon or a hammer. It does not matter how close you might be to narcissists. You could be their family or even their best friend. All they see are opportunities and advantages.

A Covert Operation

As we had talked about before, if someone displays just one or a couple of the traits above, they don't automatically fall into the narcissist category. I urge you to practice kindness tempered with love every time you judge someone. One wrong judgment could, quite possibly, forever alter the person's image in your mind.

Having said that, you might not often notice the obvious traits of narcissism in an individual. Yet, believe it or not, that person might just be a narcissist. It's quite a predicament, isn't it? It's like you are presented with a complex code to their behavior, and all you have for reference is, well, nothing. You don't know how to evaluate the person or whether they are narcissists or not. This endeavor can be quite taxing. Think about it. Do you want to play detective with a person's character every time they are in your presence or you are having a conversation with them?

So, what can you do in such a scenario?

You use the below guide.

Before that, though, let's take a quick tour through the basic elements of a covert narcissist. When understanding the covert type, you should understand that it shares the same foundational principles of the overt category; both types of narcissists lack empathy and are hungry for admiration. However, it is the presentation of such principles that differs between the two types.

Overt narcissism (or grandiose narcissism, as it is referred to in the medical community) has an outward presentation of traits. It involves people who enjoy attention and are bold and typically extroverted. They are as easy to spot as a large elephant in the middle of a busy city street. I might even go so far as to say that sometimes, their intentions—even though they try to mask them—are revealed through subtle actions or words.

On the other hand, covert narcissists are more clandestine. They don't always reveal their true intentions, masking them with shyness, self-deprecation, and social withdrawal. You might think that they are socially awkward, but in reality, they are hiding their disdain for someone else. Since they cannot display their displeasure, envy, or anger more openly, they take a few steps backward, hiding under a veneer of timidness.

It is only when you get to understand their nature that you become aware of their intentions. But that is the big question, isn't it? Just how can you understand their nature? How can you recognize a covert narcissist?

After all, covert narcissists are veterans at masking their intentions. They apply underhanded and calculated measures to get what they want. They are quite strategic in their manipulation. They may have malevolent intentions, but they are buried deep inside them, waiting to be let out.

Do you know the worst part about it all? You may never see them make a move before it is too late. After all, how could you mistrust that humble friend? Why would you suspect the socially awkward buddy of yours? You wouldn't. They just cannot possibly be narcissists, can they?

Most of the time, their actions can leave their loved ones feeling disoriented and blindsided. It's a shock. An unnatural phenomenon that their loved ones and friends would never have predicted. I would go so far as to say that they are the more dangerous of the narcissist types because they can hide their narcissism well enough to know that they can win if they play by the rules a little. They know that a fake apology might distract the viewer from their true nature. They understand the basic rules of respect, the "thank yous," "sorrys," and "take cares."

But remember what we said about respect. It isn't just about knowing what to say but how to say it. In other words, the intentions of the person matter as well. When you speak about your accomplishments, the covert narcissists aren't appreciating you because they genuinely support you; they know that to blend into society, they have to congratulate your success, if only for a little while. In the end, they care about their reputation. They might already be formulating plans to demean your character or humiliate you in some capacity.

They can carry their facade on for as long as possible. You might not even recognize their narcissistic tendencies for years if they choose to mask them for that long.

So, how can you break through their outer layers to reach the true entity residing within? You learn to recognize certain traits.

Their quiet smugness. Sure, they may not provide the verbal or personality cues that might divulge their superiority complex. They may not be an open book, but a book they are. You just need to find the right pages and passages. The message might just reveal itself to you. These hidden 'passages' of their personality are shown through nonverbal cues and aloof detachment. A condescending glare. Dismissive gestures when you are alone with them and talk about yourself. Sighs and groans when the focus turns to you. Quick to become bored when the focus is on your interests, desires, and conversations. Yawns that are impolite even though the narcissist might pretend that they harbor no ill will. So much eye-rolling that you might think their eyeballs will flop out of their sockets soon. A lack of eye contact because they cannot stand the idea that you might just look through their deceptiveness. A high degree of distractibility that makes you wonder if they are a software program gone haywire. These are just some of the reactions that can help clue you into their intentions.

They possess a certain inattentiveness or a sense of withdrawn self-centeredness. Because of this, they are adept at scanning a situation for certain criteria. If they find it uninteresting, unworthy of their attention, or flawed in some manner, then they effectively block it out. To them, that situation might as well cease to exist entirely.

They abhor criticism. To a narcissist, criticism might as well be an ancient form that has returned from the void to target them, like a Lovecraftian entity that has no purpose, save the complete annihilation of said narcissist. It does not matter how constructively you offer it. It does not matter if you have provided criticism with so much kindness that Gandhi himself would wake up from his grave to hold your hand. A narcissist will respond with sarcasm, dismissiveness, or passive-aggressiveness to any criticism. Sometimes, they might seem like they have responded well, but deep down, they feel enraged and humiliated. They are already plotting their vengeance.

Covert narcissists love to put themselves down. You might wonder about the wisdom of the above action. It is a form of emotional and mental self-harm after all. So why do covert narcissists employ it? The reality is that there is a certain tactic to their actions. According to Maury Joseph, a doctor of psychology, narcissists love to depend on others to raise and carry their self-esteem. For that to happen, they need to show that they need some form of help. Enter the low self-esteem that someone needs to boost.

Let us not forget **their tendency to hold grudges**. You might have said something, whether knowingly or unintentionally, that might offend them. They might feel as though they were not treated fairly by someone. Rather than deal with the situation at that moment, they tend to bury their displeasure deep inside them, allowing it to fester into something dangerous. They might not respond immediately, but they are plotting the many ways they can bring down the offender. They plan their revenge slowly. You might wonder how this is different from an overt narcissist. The reality is that over narcissists do hold grudges as well, but most of the time, you can see their displeasure out in the open. With covert narcissists, it might look like you are their best friend, but deep down, they don't share the same feeling.

They lack empathy. Either their empathy is so low that might be suffering an emotional drought, or their empathy is self-serving. You can try pointing it out to them. 'Try' being the operative word. As a response, the narcissist will turn the conversation on themselves, exaggerating or enhancing their problem. It might feel as though you shattered their lives so much that they are now picking up the pieces. They make their life sound like such a tragedy that the ghost of Shakespeare might write a play on their experiences. Even when they show empathy, it is merely because they are grooming you to accept their demands in the future.

They are passive-aggressive. The truth of the matter is that we, as humans, display passive-aggressive tendencies to those around us. It's part of our nature. Call it a figment of our ego. However, when it comes to narcissists, this behavior receives an upgrade. They might respond with an "of course," "absolutely," "yes," or even "okay" to your requests, ideas, or suggestions. What they actually do is, well, absolutely nothing or the bare minimum. They'll do whatever they please or just ignore everything you said entirely.

There is sensitivity, and then there is **narcissistic sensitivity**. Even a mild joke might churn the waters of revenge inside a narcissist. They might offer an idea, and you might respond with a better one. To them, such a notion is unthinkable. How could someone dare one-up them? Why would someone demean them (nobody did, but to them, everything is personal)? In quite a few cases I have come across, the narcissist won't respond for a long time to a certain behavior. Their anger piles up. Eventually, all of that pent-up aggression goes nuclear. They explode their thoughts in a fit of rage, throughout which they will constantly place themselves as the victim.

Of course, a covert narcissist's repertoire of destructive skills is not complete without what I like to call the **"unsung specialty trait**." You read that phrase here first. If you ever find anyone using it, then know its origins. Wait a minute. That was quite narcissistic of me, wasn't it? I just made you feel as though you should celebrate this spectacular achievement of naming something (which it isn't really, since psychologists and doctors far more experienced than I am have come up with better phrases, but back to the point I am trying to make). Why would you not remember me?! How could you not celebrate the name Mona Diggins?! That right there is what a covert narcissist thinks. They believe that they are so special, so ahead of their time, so one-of-a-kind, and so misunderstood that people don't see their talents and achievements. In reality, they don't make the effort required to work their way toward gaining those achievements. They feel entitled, with a hefty dose of grandiosity, to such a degree that they NEED to receive attention. They should. There is no other way. Forget all those people who have genuinely toiled throughout their lives to reach a certain status. Their efforts don't matter. What matters is that narcissists are given the attention they are due, even if such attention is not earned.

While we are on the subject of **making demands**, know that a narcissist has many to make. They want people to acknowledge them, understand them, make their demands happen, or listen to them and them only. And what do they offer in return? Nothing. Zilch. Zip. Nada. Niets. You are going to spend so much emotional, physical, and mental effort to—and this is not something I say lightly—do their bidding, that you won't realize how much you have sacrificed.

It isn't just demands that they make. They want you to **feel sorry for them**, and they are quite adept at achieving such a reaction from you. They do this by intentionally blaming themselves, even when such blame is not necessary. Most importantly, they bring themselves down no matter how great things are going. They always have something to complain about. In fact, they feel great IF you are feeling sorry for them since that means your attention is fixated on them.

But they don't just look down on themselves; they **look down on others**. That friend of yours who is completely disrespectful to waiters? Keep an eye on them (note that it might not necessarily mean they are narcissists, but look for other traits that might indicate whether they are). The person in your life who looks disdainfully at trashmen or garbage collectors? You should better evaluate their personality.

In the end, because of all their traits, it is quite difficult for them to build or maintain relationships. You might say 'obviously' to that statement, and I agree with you. With all of the traits listed above, narcissists can be difficult to get along with, let alone build any kind of connection with. However, there are a lot more intricacies that go into revealing exactly why narcissists cannot cultivate healthy relationships.

To begin with, we might have to repeat the narcissist's mantra: Everything I do and have is important while anything that belongs to others is inconsequential. Therein lies the clue to their lack of relationship-building skills. Let's take the example of social media.

Facebook. Twitter. Instagram. Reddit. These—and many other online platforms—are meant to allow people from different parts of the world to connect and form communities based on common interests. I say "meant to." Today, the social media landscape is dotted with online trolls, unnecessary conflicts, unhealthy discussions, and, of course, the excess of discrimination on practically any grounds that people can find. It is like a world within a world. But it is not a world where one finds joy, companionship, acceptance, and love. Within this world, narcissists thrive.

Now, you might wonder, how is interacting with social media proof that narcissists are not social? Does it not prove the contrary?

Researchers from the University of Florence studied the behavior of grandiose and covert narcissists, along with non-narcissists, on social media platforms (Casale et al., 2016). They wanted to understand how each group fared in their online interactions. More specifically, they wanted to find correlations between the groups and what they consider the problematic use of social networking sites (SNSs). Hundreds of volunteers were brought into the study, ensuring that they were able to get a broad perspective of the phenomenon. In the end, they found something that might surprise you. If I were to ask you right now which of the groups had the highest scores of problematic use of SNSs, then your guess might linger on grandiose or overt narcissists. But the reality paints a different picture. What the researchers found was that it was covert narcissists who had the highest score and, by extension, the higher degree of indulging in problematic SNSs activities.

Surprising, isn't it?

However, this begs the question of why. Just why do these narcissists engage in volatile interactions online, where their online goal is to unleash some of the most derogatory combinations of words in any conversation or argument? It isn't a surprise that online trolls are not just narcissists but psychopaths and sadists as well. Don't take my word for it. I have merely provided the conclusions made by psychologists years ago.

Psychologist Jennifer Golbeck says online trolls are quick to offend, exaggerate, lie, and even manipulate conscience to win an argument (Golbeck Ph.D., 2014). In many cases, Golbeck explains that trolls just make an argument to, well, just get a response. That's it. They have no clear ideas to present. All they want is to make someone feel miserable.

As to the why, psychologist Jonathan N. Stea believes that it is because of a sense of invincibility (N. Stea Ph.D., R. Psych, 2020). When someone is behind a screen, they enjoy a false sense of security. They feel like they have a mental shield, and that only opens the floodgates into some of the darker corners of their minds. They feel powerful, and this power is fueled by the reactions of people. The more negatively people react—either from anger, hurt, sadness, or frustration—the more powerful the troll gets, eager to groom those negative emotions even more.

This sense of invincibility and power is what covert narcissists enjoy. They appear shy, withdrawn, and sometimes even unassuming when in front of others. It isn't because they truly have a humble and modest personality. It is merely because they are hesitant to show their true nature, knowing full well that people won't accept them. For that reason, they turn to the online world to feel a sense of control, able to unmask themselves and present their destructive nature to the world.

Because they are so honest on social media, they cannot bring up that same honesty in the real world. Why would they? Their nature is destructive. It isn't conducive to creating healthy relationships. They would rather spend more time online where they can exert their harmful influence than in real-world relationships where they might be revealed for who they really are. It is difficult for them to form healthy relationships, and hence, most covert narcissists are not social.

A Quick Pause

Before we go any further, there is something that I would like to let you know. Please, do not stay silent when you are attacked by an online troll. You shouldn't be the quiet victim. You shouldn't suffer in silence. You are a beautiful and unique individual who deserves to be on this planet just like everyone else. You don't deserve to be harassed, bullied, humiliated, ostracized, or insulted by a troll simply because you had a different opinion, made a post, or were the next target of an online troll.

Report the post or message, even if you think nothing happens. Talk to a friend about what you felt instead of bottling up your emotions and burying them inside. Call out the troll on their behavior, pointing out just what they said and why it is wrong. If you are attacked again, then just let go. After all, the only reason the troll reacts is that you have made a valid point, and they don't like that.

There is a reason why they are called 'trolls,' referring to the hideous, slow, lazy, and giant lumbering creatures with breath so strong it could kill all crops on the planet and send us into a global food shortage. In fact, even the troll in the young fantasy book, Harry Potter, was hideous and went down in a public toilet. I suppose that can be a proper metaphor. Trolls are hideous online, and they deserve to go down in the 'toilet' of their mind. Most importantly, remember the incredible person you are, no matter what someone online tells you.

And now, we return to our regular program, why narcissists can't make proper social connections, as if that wasn't obvious enough already. It is important to understand how they work because it helps you gain a clearer picture of their personality. Besides, knowledge is power, and right now, our goal is to bring more power to you.

While engaging in harmful social media interactions might be a way to avoid social interactions, you might wonder what else they do when not facing people.

We have understood that narcissists love to feel in power. But what happens when there is no avenue to exercise that power? What if the social media aspect was taken away?

Well, they fantasize.

Covert narcissists enjoy creating elaborate fantastical places where they are the masters of the universe. In fact, according to research published in the *Journal of Clinical Psychology*, narcissists create fantasies where they achieve heroic, hostile, life-changing, and even sexual achievements (Raskin & Novacek, 1991). Their daydreams are mainly future-oriented, where they are living out their "would be" lives. They imagine that they are famous actors, extremely intelligent doctors, Superman, the president of the United States, the world's best lover and, well, you get the picture.

Sometimes, they dwell on the past. In those instances, they reenact past scenarios where things did not go the way they had wanted them to. In their 'revised' version of events, they are the ones in control, saying the right things and taking the proper actions. The situation plays out so well in their head, that it might as well be a script to a movie. Narcissists tend to revisit these scenarios as often as they like.

Keep in mind, though, that sometimes, even non-narcissists try to relive memories. It might be because past events caused them trauma or evoked deep emotions such as shame, helplessness, anger, sadness, or any of the plethora of negative emotions that human beings carry. In some ways, this can be a coping mechanism. The point at which these trips down memory lane can be dangerous is when the memory visits impact normal life. People might live so much in their heads that they forget how to live in the world. They begin to enjoy their imaginary life so much that their real one takes a toll. They begin to procrastinate heavily. They become disillusioned with life. Depression might strike them. When harmful mental stimuli and influences affect their lives, it is a sign that they have to stop residing within the dark and turbulent confines of their minds.

It isn't just to satisfy their craving for power that the covert narcissists delve deep into their fantasies. Social media and their imaginary worlds are just two of many avenues that covert narcissists use to indulge in their power fantasies. Other avenues include joining cliques where they can exercise their power, consuming books and media that support their ideas, and even doing activities that allow them to feel superior.

All of their endeavors are established to support their self-important personas. For them to maintain their personas, one of the motivators of their actions is confirmation bias.

What exactly is confirmation bias?

Imagine that your friend came to you and, in a fit of April Fool's madness, jokes about the fact that aliens have landed on Earth. However, you take this message seriously. You start bringing out the tin-foil hat and preparing your secret bunker. Your friends and family, obviously concerned, inform you that it was all just a joke. Nothing to worry about. No brain harvesting. No butt probing. Nothing weird is going to happen to you. But you refuse to believe them.

In your mind, aliens exist, and no amount of convincing will change that idea.

That right there is confirmation bias. There is such a strong desire for your beliefs to be true that you refuse to believe any opposing thoughts or ideas. You become fixated on your ideas.

Now, this isn't necessarily a bad thing. A healthy dose of confirmation bias helps to stay focused on your goals. You might believe that you can achieve great things if you focus your attention on a certain goal. People might try to dissuade you, but you are firm in your expectations surrounding your hard work. You want to put all you can into your work to reap the best rewards. In such and many more scenarios, confirmation bias can be a fairly good psychological tool to possess.

It becomes a problem when your beliefs are twisted and nothing can change your mind. You see, covert narcissists believe that they are doing nothing wrong. This is why they can become defensive easily. It isn't that they don't want to see the error of their ways; the reality is that they simply don't think there is an error in the first place. This conviction about their actions allows them to maintain their personas. In their eyes, they are just like everybody else. There is nothing wrong with their actions. They don't believe that they are capable of causing harm. On the contrary, they believe that others are causing them harm. They are the victims, not the people they manipulate, insult, abuse, and control. No way. That is not the truth in the covert narcissist's eyes.

This confirmation bias is why they join cliques so they can exercise their power. In such groups, no one questions their ideas or actions. People support them or believe them easily, which gives the narcissists a sense of control. The books they read support their theories. Activities are tailor-made to fit their idea or lifestyle.

For example, if you were at a sporting center and invited a narcissist to go bowling, which they are not good at, they might instead draw your attention to a game of pool, which they might be fairly comfortable playing. This isn't just a matter of being uninterested in one game. Narcissists make it a point to show their displeasure with joining someone for a fun game of bowling. Even though the others might not be that good, narcissists are not thinking of simply having a great time with their friends; they are concerned about being the dominant one in the room.

You could say that life is one big competition for them. Even during moments of tranquility, they have to look for ways to one-up others. Are you in a cafe and did you order a unique latte with a fancy name? Watch out for the narcissist who wants to show that their drink is fancier than yours. Having a conversation about a movie—like *Inception* for example—where you provide your thoughts on the movie? You guessed it; narcissists are going to show off their repository of knowledge to prove that they are right about the movie's meanings, theories, and symbolism, even if they have to pull reasons out of thin air and without much thought.

Because they are cooped up in their fantasy or mental bubble, they don't much care for anyone outside of said bubble. If you would like to enter their domain, then know that they are the masters of everything, even things where they have no knowledge, skill, or experience.

What happens to those who do not adhere to their rules? Well, they are ignored. Narcissists can develop a nonchalant disregard for anyone who does not recognize them in a certain manner or follow specific rules. They might stand you up, showing you that they don't care for your time or that you are nothing but a triviality to them. If you call them, they might wait until the last moment to respond. Invite them over and they might deliberately be late. Even if you are with them, they pretend that they are not paying attention just to show you that what you think or say does not matter.

Why would it? After all, *you* should be listening to *them*. God forbid if you have a better idea or reason than them. That could never happen in the world we live in. Or should we say, in the world that *they* live in.

While we are on the topic of personal thoughts and ideas, let us not forget about your talents or abilities. It does not matter what you can do. It does not exist in the eyes of the narcissist. If they find out that you are better than them at something, then off they go using all of the weapons in their arsenal against you. They will deliberately ignore you or take advantage of your time. They might go back to seeing their groups or cliques or doing things that feed their confirmation biases. They might even jump into the online world just to show their superiority and ruin some unlucky person's moment.

Phew! It is already exhausting just reading about a narcissist, isn't it? Well, we are just getting started. Being well-versed in their lives is important. Knowing about their habits can make the difference between identifying them in time or falling for their victim mentality.

Before we delve even deeper into the world of narcissists, I would like to provide a small checklist. This checklist will allow you to identify if your friend is indeed a narcissist or not. In the table, you will find a list of behavioral patterns. Using the 'Existence' column, add a yes to any behavior that you think applies to your friend. Remember, this is just a simple test to better understand your friend. It isn't a narcissistic evaluation checklist and should not be considered as such. My goal here is to help you recognize patterns that can help you identify the kind of relationship you have with your friend. Is it healthy? Are there signs of manipulation? Do you think emotional abuse is present in your relationship?

Behavioral Patterns	Existence (Yes or No)
Feels superior and is condescending toward others	
Shows passive-aggressiveness	
Victim mentality	
Judges others and is overly critical, typically from the sidelines or behind someone's back	
Low self-awareness and does not introspect when you point out faults	
Has a distaste for straightforwardness and honesty or avoids them entirely	
Indulges in harmful gossip	

Stonewalls you when discussing difficult topics or questions	
Dismisses others' feelings	
Expects you to be a constant caretaker	
Rules do not apply to them, and they might often break them without reason	
Pries and prods into your affairs, even after you have told them not to do so	
Tarnishes the reputation and image of others, sometimes for petty reasons	
Does not follow codes of conduct, often stepping on others' toes, crossing personal space, and invading boundaries	
Humble bragging or false	

humility	
Pays heavy attention to appearance	
Feels entitled to an unhealthy degree	
Shows contempt and rage, usually in private and sometimes over trivial matters	
Prone to usage of flattery simply to get what they want	
Struggles with decision-making	
Targets other people's problems and issues, often becoming uncomfortably curious about them	
Double-standards	
Grudges never diminish over time	

Plots or takes revenge against people, even over trivial matters	
Unfair in how they deal with people (For example, they expect kindness but do not reciprocate in kind, no pun intended)	
Capable of faking illnesses, injuries, and even physical or mental conditions to draw attention to themselves	
Uses the vulnerability of others to their advantage, typically for exploitative purposes	
Sarcastic and cynical when not required	
Demands are unreasonable	
Blames others for their mistakes	
Not hesitant in belittling	

others	

A Quick Note

Think about how you are diagnosing someone since some traits might not necessarily indicate narcissism. For example, a person might use flattery to get something from others. You might have done it too. Does that make you a narcissist? No, because non-narcissists do not enjoy the act. They make up for their actions in the future or even offer an apology. In the case of a narcissist, they enjoy the feeling of being able to trick someone. It gives them a certain rush, which they seek to replenish over and over again.

Even better would be to go through the next section, where you are given a more in-depth look at the way a narcissist functions. The strategies that narcissists use, whether overt or covert, will give you an idea of what to expect and how to deal with it.

The Tactician

Narcissists have a robust toolbox of tricks that they can quickly use for various situations. In many cases, the experience they have gained using their techniques allows them to adapt to a situation. Often, you might not know what they are up to unless you are aware of these techniques.

Here are some of their tactics.

Narcissists covet something you may hold or possess, such as your accomplishments, intelligence, looks, courage, possessions, or even resources. A twisted form of reasoning in their mind allows them to conclude that you are somehow linked to the things that they lack, which you currently have. That's when they use a sneaky tool known as a **mixed put-down**. Their goal with this tactic is to bring down someone from their pedestal while also avoiding accountability for their actions. They want to attack someone without making it obvious. Their goal is to clear the space previously occupied by their victim and take it over.

For example, they attempt to make someone look inept so that when the attack is successful and the victim is feeling vulnerable, they can step in to sound more knowledgeable or intelligent.

A mixed put-down occurs when the narcissist marries a compliment with an insult. They might say, "That dress looks fantastic on you. All you need is to lose that belly fat, and you are good to go." Alternatively, they could start with the insult and then move on to the compliment. You might have heard a variation of, "You know that you are not supposed to do that, right? Well, at least you have put in a lot of work, so that's good."

They usually try to make their words seem innocuous. Their experience using a mixed put-down helps them phrase their sentences better, giving you barely enough hints to realize that you have just been attacked, so you have no idea why you are feeling helpless, vulnerable, or sometimes even guilty. Over time, these feelings evolve, and you unconsciously find yourself seeking the narcissist's approval.

Double meanings are used more by covert narcissists, although grandiose narcissists also employ them when they have to. With this tactic, the classic adage of "say what you mean and mean what you say" takes on a whole twisted form. However, it is the illusion that they want to present to you. They want you to think that the meaning behind their words is obvious and holds no hidden intentions.

Here is one phrase that you might have heard and that might have sent mixed signals running through your mind, "Looks like you have it all figured out." On one hand, it might sound harmless. Question the narcissist's intentions and they will more than likely respond by saying that they were merely admiring your intellect. What it really is, however, is a dangerous blend of sarcasm and condescension. The narcissist dislikes your ability to figure things out, so they mock you indirectly. At the same time, they want to show you that you have not done anything special.

Then there are the **coded messages**, which might just be the most dangerous tactic of the three we have discussed so far. A coded message is named so because it is an idea or knowledge that only you and the narcissist are aware of. The narcissist wants to make you feel small in front of others. They might make a casual comment or throw in a joke about something that could offend you, is fairly personal to you, or is a sensitive matter. Nobody else knows about this vulnerability except you and the narcissist. To the others, whatever the narcissist says might sound like a lighthearted comment. Yet you are left feeling embarrassed, hurt, and offended. Perhaps even shocked. The narcissist wants to undermine you. It is their way of saying, "See? Don't try to be better than me because I know all your secrets."

Narcissists also employ the art of **diversion**. In this tactic, they can easily switch between loving admiration and disapproval. You are constantly kept on your toes. The narcissist, on the other hand, wants to hide the idea that they are trying to blame you for something. Their disapproval means that you have done something wrong, even though in reality, you might not have. I would argue that perhaps you might have done everything well without a single mistake. This does not sit well with the narcissist, and they blame you for an error, whether that error is real or imagined. Once you are sufficiently guilty, they switch and display affection, throwing you off. You then start to blame yourself. How could you make such a horrible mistake when someone so loving is supporting you? Why couldn't you just do it right in the first place? What is wrong with you? From there, it keeps getting worse until you simply blame yourself for nearly everything that goes wrong.

What if the narcissist is unable to attack you? As an example, you could be in the presence of family. The narcissist might not be able to say or do anything without being called out. They can't say anything about you that your family won't be able to deny. What do they do then? The narcissist develops a **tunnel-vision** tactic, where they zoom in on something insipid or irrelevant to draw the attention away from you. Your family might be in awe, recollecting your recent accomplishment. Instead of joining in, the narcissist might try to change the subject to the weather, the latest movies, or anything else that does not involve you.

But what if they need something more potent to use? They resort to **shaming**. Shame can be such a debilitating emotion to experience. You feel as though your worth has just taken the elevator straight to the basement levels of your confidence. Once there, it digs a six-foot hole and leaps into it. The result is that you end up thinking that you are not that great, talented, smart, successful, or good at something. One of the ways that narcissists shame you is by using an approach known as "historical revisionism." The narcissist will deliberately recall a moment from the past that is meant to highlight the fact that you are less special than you currently are. If you ask them about it, then they might say that they were merely talking about the rise of your success or your "humble beginnings."

If you suddenly decide to confront the narcissist and talk about their behavior, then you are in for a world of mental roller-coaster trips. In any healthy relationship, there is always room for amicable disagreements or respectful discussion. You are free to express yourself and allow the other person to do so as well. A good friend absorbs everything with an air of understanding. Not a narcissist. They use a technique known as **gaslighting**.

In this technique, the narcissist tries to convince you that your cognizance of the abuse, manipulation, or mental games that they subject you to is not real or is inaccurate. They intentionally devalue your feedback. They will aim to invalidate your theories. Your emotions will be criticized. They might even go through something known as "abuse amnesia," where they deny doing any wrong to you. "The only reason I did it was because of what you did," "That did not happen the way you said it," "I said it casually while you became too sensitive about it so that's not *my* problem," and "You took it way more seriously than what I intended." These are just some of the phrases that they use. The result is that you begin to doubt yourself. All of a sudden, you are questioning your approach. Even if your doubts are small, they are more than enough to slowly grow in your mind, like fungus latching on to old food; eventually, your mind is going to be too infected with self-doubts.

This is also one of the reasons why victims end up suffering even after they have cut ties with the narcissist or ended relationships with them. The mental invalidation that the victims receive is so potent that they feel weak to defend their perceptions and agencies. In many cases, this very sense of self-doubt compels the victims to stay in a relationship because they are constantly blaming themselves to a point where they refuse to accept the emotional danger they are in.

Even if you happen to find a way to confront them, the narcissist will **lie** or **deny** your points. Sometimes, they even resort to half-truths where they admit to one thing but then reject another. Typically, the fact they agree on is milder than the one they lie about. For example, if you let the narcissist know that they have been getting angry with you for trivial reasons, then they might agree to the anger but then add a lie. They might say that they were trying to have a proper conversation with you, but you kept rejecting them, which caused them to lose their temper. They have effectively presented their honesty, which lulls you into believing their lie as well. If they cannot convince you, then they simply deny anything you have to say.

When they cannot deny, they simply evade the topic through **avoidance**. They might say that they refuse to talk about the topic, citing a busy schedule, a sudden presence of a migraine, or any other excuse they can conjure at that moment. However, in many cases, the narcissist uses avoidance to gain some time to think about a rebuttal. They haven't entirely forgotten your words. They are merely buying time to gain an advantage.

In some situations, the narcissist might not resort to a simple conversation. They might use **intimidation** tactics to get the reaction that they want, which is typically fear or helplessness. Narcissists can intimidate directly, using phrases such as "You're never going to have a better life without me," "You will lose, no matter what happens," or even "You have no idea what I am capable of."

Alternatively, they can use indirect intimidation by either using a real-life story to allude to something or their past to make themselves seem bigger. "Check out this news. Apparently, this guy tried to end his seven years of friendship because he thought the friend was manipulating him. The friend ended up taking everything and moving to another country. Man, some people don't learn." Here, they are trying to let their victim know that if something were to happen to them, they would probably take the victim's possessions.

Let's take another example. "I have always been a fighter. When I was young, I almost killed somebody because that dude said some terrible things about me." Here, you probably notice the implied threat. If you confront the narcissist about their words, then they feign ignorance and innocence saying that they were just trying to make conversation.

Looking at all of the tactics that narcissists use, one might wonder how a relationship with a narcissist might look. It is good to know the finer details of what they are capable of, but it is equally important to have a broader view of the relationship since that allows you to see how the different pieces of a narcissist's personality come together.

A Sinking Ship

A narcissistic relationship is highly toxic. It is an accumulation of abuse (whether physical or emotional), lies, deceit, manipulation, intimidation, and the gradual breakdown of the victim's mental strength. In the relationship, you will probably find that:

- You face condescension for no reason.
- Sex is a power-play where they resort to gaslighting you if they do not perform or you do not meet their sexual demands.
- If you are sick, they are quick to anger as though they are the ones who are affected and not you.

- They ignore your requests or just forget about them.
- Your friendship is based on favors, where you are the one helping the narcissist while receiving nothing in return.
- Your attention should be on them. They try to isolate you from other friends so that they can become a dominant presence in your life.
- They enjoy creating conflicts between people. This is either because of the previous reason, where they want the victim to be dependent on them, or simply because they enjoy feeling powerful.
- No matter what happens, they often resort to silent treatments, attacking your conscience. You end up feeling guilty to such a degree that you are pleading with them for forgiveness.
- They offer little in the way of respect or understanding. In fact, you should be the one to understand their emotions.
- If they have issues or faults, they project those issues onto you. It might seem as though you are the one who needs help, not them.
- You feel exhausted. Often, you might find yourself not having the energy to do anything that you want to do. Your time is spent tending to the narcissist's demands.
- You have so much to lose, yet so little to gain.
- Their happiness is your goal, and they do not attempt to make you happy.

- If someone asks you questions about the narcissist, then you might provide a lot of details. However, if the same person asks questions about you to the narcissist, you shouldn't be surprised to find that no answers are forthcoming. It is as though your identity, likes, dislikes, passions, goals, dreams, and hopes are inconsequential.
- If they ever raise your confidence or build you up, then there is a high chance that they are planning to chip away at it in the future or use it to their advantage.

For example, they might constantly encourage you to be honest about them. You might do so, and in the beginning, all might seem well. It is when you tell them a difficult truth in the future that they turn your confidence against you. They might mention how you are crass and arrogant, have no concern for people's feelings, or anything else to demolish the confidence you have grown.

- Beware the alienation. Narcissists might talk horribly about you, your family, friends, and people you know.

In most scenarios, they do this in incremental levels of honesty and intensity. For example, they might start by pointing out minor faults. They might even forgive you for those faults, as though they are an angel from the heavens with a halo hovering over their head. You might start believing their forgiving nature, thinking how lucky you are to have them as a friend. Over time, they begin to make harsher observations. You, smitten with their angelic personality, begin to look at those close to you. You dissect their personality, looking for flaws in everything. Do they smile properly? Are they behaving well outdoors? Did they sound selfish that one time they asked for extra sugar from the barista for their triple-mocha caramel grande? Aren't they ashamed of themselves?

The above questions are just some of the cancerous ideas that begin to spread through your mind, eating away at the confidence, beliefs, hopes, dreams, and anything else you value about your near and dear ones. You might slowly start giving up the people whom you value because you simply want the narcissist—whom you are close to worshipping like a divine being—to admire you. That right there is what the narcissist had been waiting for the whole time. Because at that point, they are ready to take over your life. And you have no one to call.

- To a narcissist, it is their way or the highway. They don't care about your way of seeing things. What matters is what opinions they hold.

- You might always look for ways to meet the friend, even when you simply want to spend time by yourself. Often, you feel a sense of anxiety before you meet them and might experience exhaustion when you are with them.

- You might feel as though most—if not all—moments you spend with the narcissist are a competition. They are trying to one-up you at every opportunity they get. Did you have a bad day? Wait till you hear their horrible story, which just happens to be worse than yours. Have you accomplished something in your personal life? It doesn't matter. The narcissist coincidentally happens to have a better accomplishment.

Magnetic Energy

I know how things might look to you. After reading everything I have put into this book so far, I wouldn't blame you if you feel as though you are a truly unlucky person. After all, I felt that way as well. I had a narcissistic friend and eventually—as though life wanted to throw one more 'gotcha!' moment at me—found a narcissistic husband at the doorstep of my life, all gift-wrapped with the most elegant ribbon you could find.

I felt unlucky. I felt cheated out of the good things in life. I can still clearly recollect a moment I had with my beautiful first-born. He was just a little over a year old when he would begin crawling around the house.

Watching him, I saw what a blessing I had received. Which immediately made me realize that this blessing came from a curse of a partner. As soon as I imagined that, I was shocked. Never had I encouraged such thoughts.

It was too late. The dam had burst open. With that, I allowed the tears to flow freely down my face and stain the comfortable pants I wore at home.

After that moment, I decided that I would not pay attention to the misfortunes that I had faced in life. They pale in comparison to the wonderful and fortunate moments I have experienced, such as the birth of my child. Nothing and no one can take that away from me.

However, I also had to come to terms with a harsh truth; I was a narcissist magnet.

Thankfully, I was able to keep the number of narcissists in my life to a bare minimum (apart from my friend and husband, I know one more, but I have cut ties with her).

I would like you to take a look around you with renewed knowledge. Try examining the people in your life and see if they have narcissistic tendencies. Don't be quick to judge. Take your time evaluating their personalities, actions, and words. Remember that while you are trying to understand them better, they might continue to attack or influence you. Learn to protect and defend yourself. I will teach you how to do so in chapters 4 and 5. For now, let us figure out if you have more narcissists in your life than you need.

At this point, you might have to answer a question. Just how much is too much? How many narcissists do you need to have to reach a certain threshold? What is the maximum number of narcissistic individuals you need in your life before you lose all control over yourself?

The truth is that there is no certain limit. Even one narcissist can ruin your life, so don't wait for it to reach four or five before you realize that you have had enough. I don't think you need to have more than one narcissist in your life. By that, I don't mean you remove anyone who displays a certain tendency toward narcissism; we all do. I am talking about toxic narcissists who fall into either the grandiose or covert category.

Let's return to you. More specifically, why you might have more than one narcissist in your life. The fundamental idea is that narcissists are primarily attracted to four kinds of people. Let me also offer you a kicker; they don't always target the vulnerable and docile. Contrary to what most people have been telling me, I have noticed that narcissists also enjoy latching on to talented, successful, and even strong-willed people.

In all honesty, I would never say that narcissists have only one criterion for their victims. There are a lot of factors to take into consideration. The narcissist's lifestyle, ambitions, goals, and even preferences—all of these factors decide the kind of person each narcissist targets.

However, to gain a broad perspective, there are four main groups of victims.

The first group of people features those who are **impressive** in a certain area of their lives. Perhaps they are highly successful. Maybe they are so wealthy that buying a sports car is like booking an Uber. Or—in the eyes of the narcissist—the potential victim might have a splendid family, career, friend circle, talents, or achievements. They want to link themselves to the lives of such people, easing their way into a close relationship. What they truly seek is control over the people's lives and their impressive possessions.

The second group of people is made up of those who can make the narcissists **feel good about themselves**. This group provides the actions, words, and gestures that the narcissists crave. In many cases, victims become dependent on pleasing the abuser, often going to great lengths to get a reaction.

In the third group, we are looking at people who are **ardent supporters** of the narcissist. This group includes anyone capable of defending the abuser in front of other people. They deny any presence of abuse, defend the narcissist to an unhealthy degree, and constantly provide justifications for the negative emotions that they experience. They are capable of validating the narcissist's emotions and feelings, won't leave the abuser despite how horrible things might become, and even overlook the abuser's flaws.

Finally, we are looking at those people who can make the narcissist **look better when they are in front of others**. This means that through mere association, people automatically assume that the abuser's personality is similar to the victim's. For example, an individual might be extremely kind and generous. That individual's friends, family, and close ones are aware of that. When people see the narcissist in the presence of said individual, they automatically think only positive ideas. They would never imagine that deep down, a darkness is waiting to be unleashed.

If you fall into any of these categories, you might be at a risk of attracting narcissists, or you might be able to explain why there are so many in your life right now. There are a lot of nuances that go into each group. For example, people may be ardent supporters of narcissists due to certain connections. I have seen people support their family members, who are clearly displaying narcissistic tendencies, simply because they refuse to accept the alternative. No matter what one says, the truth is blocked. As you can see, familial bonds are difficult to ignore. People can go through years of abuse without catching on to what is happening to them.

You might also attract narcissists if you are an empath. The word empath is thrown around a lot, often with metaphysical attachments. However, at its fundamental level, empaths are people who can "tune into" the emotions of others. They are emotional sponges, able to understand people on a much deeper level. Typically, they are sensitive and timid. In other words, they are the perfect target for narcissists who can take advantage of their sensitivity to manipulate and control them. Empaths are also particularly vulnerable because they are quite understanding and empathetic to a high degree. They usually try to reach out to the person in anguish (and yes, they end up considering the narcissist to be someone who needs help). While the intentions of empaths are rainbows and unicorns, the ones of narcissists are twisted monstrosities straight from the pages of H.P. Lovecraft.

While it is important to understand how narcissism manifests in people, I believe that it is equally vital to recognize just how narcissism works. For that, we are going to delve deeper into the psychological condition, working our way from its spectrum to its qualities.

Chapter 2:

A Deeper Look at

Narcissism

I am a beautiful human being.

While we are on the subject of beauty, there is a tale of a man who was born as a result of a union between a god and a nymph. This man was beautiful and striking. Such was his beauty that many fell in love with him instantly. You could say that it was love at first sight. What a sight he was!

For his part, the man showed nothing but disdain and contempt toward his admirers as though they were somehow beneath him.

This man was Narcissus.

One fine day, Narcissus was walking through a forest when he felt a presence following him. The shadowy figure would not reveal itself, so Narcissus continued on this journey. Eventually, the figure revealed itself to be Echo, an Oread nymph. She practically threw herself upon him, trying to win his attention. After a failed attempt at trying to hug him (which I think is fairly inappropriate), Narcissus rejected her and went on his way. Echo was so grief-stricken that she wandered the forest for the rest of her life, eventually wilting away until nothing was left of her but a sound that would carry on.

That, my friends, is a short history of the word echo.

Oh wait, that wasn't the point, was it?

Well, there is more to it. Nemesis, the goddess of revenge, decided to punish Narcissus. She guided him to a clear pool, where he gazed upon a beautiful sight. He was in love! Finally, he had found someone beautiful enough to deserve his feelings.

Except, that 'person' was his own reflection. Unable to understand why the other presence did not reciprocate Narcissus's feelings, the beautiful man ended up taking his own life, leading to an ugly twist in his story.

The story is often used to describe the behavior of narcissists since they are so focused on themselves that they completely ignore the feelings and emotions of others. Their victims are usually unaware of their tactics. However, with enough awareness, people can look out for the signs of abuse, manipulation, deceit, lies, and control and take measures to avoid them. I think at this point, you might be able to recognize the narcissist in your life quite easily.

But before you start making any diagnosis, there is a depth to narcissism that you should know.

We have discussed the different types of narcissism. But do we know its intensity?

By identifying the two different types of narcissists, we can recognize them using the traits of each type. However, it is equally important to know that there is severity to the degree of narcissism.

As I mentioned before, everyone is a narcissist. We are all proud of ourselves, toot our own horn on occasions, manipulate the feelings of others to get what we want (albeit not in a harmful manner and we don't feel a sense of glee due to our actions), and lie to the people close to us. There is no denying that.

Does that mean that we should be worried about our personality?

Not necessarily. Despite the existence of narcissism in all of us, we know that we would never allow it to become a dangerous tool. We don't begin to destroy lives, cause pain and suffering, or slowly degrade someone's confidence and character.

It is clear, then, that narcissism falls on a spectrum (Krizan & Herlache, 2017). Most people are somewhere in the middle. A small percent of the population falls on either side of the spectrum. The ones you should watch out for are those who fall on the higher end of the narcissism spectrum, whether they adopt the grandiose category or the covert one.

When narcissism ventures into the dangerous end of the spectrum, we have a case of narcissistic personality disorder (NPD). Once again, I would like you to be very careful when you decide that someone has NPD. Just because you dislike someone or the person has some traits you are not fond of does not mean you can conclude that the person has NPD. It is not only unfair to the individual, but it is also unethical. Even if you do come to that conclusion, be even more careful about spreading that information to others. That right there could be very dangerous. It could permanently destroy someone's reputation or worse, their lives.

To truly recognize narcissistic behavior, let us look at what narcissism is.

Most victims often ask a simple question that holds many layers of complexity: Why?

Just why are narcissists the way they are? What caused them to become people with so many negative ideas and traits? What kind of tragedy must they have faced?

While it is tempting to have a sympathetic approach to narcissism, I recommend having a rational stance on the subject. I understand that past traumas often decide how people might turn out, but that still does not excuse their actions. When a narcissist causes irreparable damage to someone's psyche, then it does not matter what extreme pain and abuse they themselves might have faced; what matters more is that they are destroying someone's life. I know that might seem fairly cruel. However, my main goal here is to help give you the knowledge and tools to protect yourself. Once you are in a safe area in your mind, you can then decide how you would like to approach the narcissist.

One of the reasons for narcissism is the **environment** that people grow up in. You might think that abuse is the sole reason for a narcissist's behavior. That is just one side of the coin. On the other side is the presence of excessive attention and adoration. Children need attention and adoration from their parents, but at the same time, they also require guidance. If the parents are not able to teach the difference between right and wrong, children grow up to become adults who believe that they can enforce their own right and wrong benchmarks on the world around them. That does not mean that parents have to be too strict with their children. Excessive criticism can lower a child's feelings of self-worth. They begin to work hard to impress their parents, and the areas they focus on become their life's work. When they grow up to be adults, they cannot stand any form of advice or criticism in those specific areas.

NOTE: Bear in mind that while some children may develop narcissism, it does not necessarily mean they are going to be manipulative adults. It might just be a typical phase in their growth. Children have to explore emotions to fully understand them. When you look at a child crying loudly in a public space, don't be quick to judge them. They have yet to understand what it means to behave in a particular manner when in public.

It has also been theorized that **neurobiology and genetics** can play a part in narcissism (Mayo Clinic Staff, 2017). This comes as no surprise as there are studies that link genes to various mental health issues, including bipolar disorder. However, further studies are required to add more concrete proof to the theories.

Finally, the **environment** can also play a vital role in developing narcissism. Environmental factors could include various things, from the schools children attend to the neighborhoods people grow up in to even workplace environments that breed unhealthy competition. It is important to note that narcissism isn't gained overnight despite the environmental factors. It is a slow growth that takes place over months and sometimes even years.

Get the Measurements Right

Knowing that various factors contribute to narcissism is just one part of the process. The next part is measuring the degree of narcissism that a person has. Remember, we are talking about a spectrum. You and everyone else can fall on various points of the spectrum. You could have a mild version of narcissism while others—such as a friend—might be on the dangerous end.

How can we find out? Is there a tool or aid that we can use to check the intensity of narcissism?

There is. It is called the Narcissistic Personality Inventory (NPI).

The NPI is a self-assessment questionnaire that features 40 statements that appear in pairs. Each pair features questions that depict two opposite observations. One statement provides a certain criterion, while the second statement is the antithesis of the first. For example, one statement mentions that you are quite natural at being influential, while its partner statement specifies that you are not good at influencing people. People then have to choose which of the two statements applies to them.

The higher they score on the test, the closer they are to having toxic narcissistic tendencies such as aggressiveness, feelings of superiority, a tendency to either cause emotional or physical abuse (or both), and immoderate levels of arrogance. The questionnaire also aims to identify some of the more hidden components of narcissism, some of which include the aim to be exploitative, feelings of entitlement, and delusions of grandeur.

The NPI uses a scoring system with 40 being the highest and 0 being the lowest. However, the chance of reaching a single-digit number is extremely rare, and getting a 0 either means that the person is a strange phenomenon, or they are lying, which by itself might indicate a certain level of narcissism. Scoring low means that, while the person may have low levels of narcissism, they also suffer from self-esteem issues. They might not have harmful intentions, but they need to work on building their confidence. People who fall on the other extreme level might have high levels of psychopathy.

No, you did not read that wrong. A high score on the questionnaire predicts psychopathy. However, it is wrong to confuse the kind of psychopathy the questionnaire predicts with the ones you see on TV. A narcissist does not necessarily become Dr. Hannibal Lecter. There is a world of difference between the two, and it is quite dangerous to enter the questionnaire with the mentality that someone with a high score might be hiding dead bodies in their garden.

I once met someone who had toured the world and started her own motivation business. She seemed to have a natural charisma. She had a great command of the stage and was a wonderful conversationalist. Initially, she had her own social media account, but she grew from there. She began to reach more and more people, always growing her audience until she was able to have her own show.

However, it became obvious that she was lying about a lot of the things that she had claimed. Apparently, she had met a successful entrepreneur on one of her trips, when it was discovered that she had bought tickets to his show. She had been in India for a couple of weeks, yet according to her, she had spent a considerable time in a monastery to understand peace and tranquility. She had even faked an injury to postpone a show just so she could complete her holiday in Bali.

One has to be bold to spin such grand tales that serve mainly to be self-aggrandizing. More importantly, one has to detach themselves from their conscience to carry the lie forward for as long as necessary. While she did not have a psychological examination, I visited a psychologist friend of mine to understand this behavior. The businesswoman I had mentioned had clear signs of psychopathy.

But was she a serial killer? Did she stalk the nights looking for victims? Not at all.

That is something we have to understand about psychology. Rarely can you take one diagnosis and run with it to form your own conclusions. There are numerous factors, spectrums, and criteria to consider before forming a conclusion. After all, a wrong diagnosis could destroy a person. Imagine walking up to someone and telling them that they are a psychopath because of a few traits. Think about the devastation your words could create on the person's psyche, forever convincing them they are a potential risk to people around them.

If you constantly look at people behind bars and the wanted news on TV, then you are going to find dangerous psychopaths. But that is confirmation bias (and we know how harmful that can be). Reality is nuanced. According to some estimates, 10% of the people who are employed in the financial sector are psychopaths (Silver, 2012). If you are an accountant, I truly apologize for that statement, but you are not necessarily part of that 10%. Moreover, even the people in the 10% are not masked mad people hell-bent on causing mayhem. Contrary to popular belief, only a small percentage of psychopaths are violent.

However, what psychopathy means is that people are prone to commit morally wrong actions and that they are aware of it. It is just that they don't care. Psychopaths lie, cheat, deceive, and enjoy hurting others. They employ abuse to gain a level of control.

Sound familiar? Of course. The conditions that define psychopathy closely mirror those of narcissism. It is for this reason that narcissists (of the extreme kind) are often considered psychopaths.

If you would like for your friend or someone you know to take the test, then you just have to visit this website: openpsychometrics.org/tests/NPI/.

Do you think 40 questions is a bit too much? Then how about one?

Researchers at Ohio State University realized that there might be an easier way to find out if someone is a narcissist (Ohio State News, 2014). You just have to ask people.

No, I am not pulling your leg. If you are looking at this page with a bewildered expression, then I can understand your reaction. After all, you might never imagine that decades of research into the human mind finally yielded an incredible solution, to simply ask the narcissist if they are a narcissist. That does not sound like progress. In fact, it might not even sound smart. You might wonder why no one had thought about it before.

The reality is that people had tried that approach. Yet the reason it works in present times is because of the wealth of knowledge that we already have about narcissism. The important part about the approach is not whether someone admits to being a narcissist or not; the true value of the question lies in the answers that you might receive. Paying special care to what the person says divulges much about them.

This approach works by posing a simple statement to the person and asking them to rate themselves. You also need to provide a few additional details. Here is the statement:

I am a narcissist.

You then add this information: **Note that the term narcissist refers to characteristics like vanity, high ego, and self-focus.**

After you have provided the statement and the additional information, you offer a scale from 1 to 7, where 1 means the statement is not true and 7 means the statement is true.

Researchers have various ideas on why this technique might work. One of the reasons that they lean toward is the growing freedom of expression around the world. The internet has given the space for people to showcase their personalities regardless of what they may be. In today's virtual world, narcissistic personalities don't just receive support; they receive followers as well. All you have to do is browse through YouTube or Instagram to know what I am talking about. There are plenty of content creators and influencers who are known to brandish their wealth in the public eye and openly display condescending behavior. You would be surprised to know that these online personalities are sometimes considered inspiration.

We live in a world where narcissism is an aspiration. That reason encourages anyone to openly accept the fact that they are narcissists. Asking them a direct question might just provide you with a direct answer.

Once you know that your friend might be a narcissist, it is time to recognize what they are capable of. To know that, we need to dive deeper into the qualities that make up a narcissist.

Quality Matters

We know that narcissists are pathological liars capable of spewing fantastical excuses and tales just to get what they want. We are aware of the fact that they can exaggerate to extreme degrees simply because they want to gain higher ground or superiority. They love to show off, take credit where it is not due (and sometimes for other people's work), and engage in various self-aggrandizing behaviors.

Because they are constantly trying to create a better image of themselves, they don't like it when something threatens that image. This could include criticism or advice. They become aggressive, choosing to either engage in conflict (verbal or physical) or evacuate the premises immediately. They also try to make a scene while they are leaving in an attempt to let everyone around them know that someone offended them. You might notice them sulking off, walking over to someone else to complain, or just storming out in fury.

However, what I would like to focus on are some of the qualities that are not commonly known.

Let's talk about the fact that they either prefer **exploitative or superficial relationships**. Narcissists project a false image of themselves to the world. It's like wearing a mask and costume and considering that to be the real version. Their image of themselves is idealized based on what they would like to be, achieve, have, or even believe. It is this image they want people to recognize. They do not want their true self revealed to the world.

As a result, when they enter relationships, they place numerous conditions and criteria that are almost like rules. They want their partners and friends to recognize this image they have created, not the actual person. They, in turn, look at the surface-level characteristics of people. If someone has a trait that is useful to them, they pursue a friendship with that person. People are given a value based on how beneficial they can be. You shouldn't be surprised that after they have formed relationships with others, they are not wary of boundaries. They find reasons to step on other people's toes and cross their boundaries. However, they expect the other person to give them space and allow them to do whatever they want without question.

Because they are honing in on the usefulness of people, they completely disregard the human beneath all of the traits they seek. In short, they **don't have empathy** for others, or if they do, it is minimal and only used when they want to emotionally manipulate their victims. They also invalidate the emotions of others, disregarding people's wants, needs, and desires.

While they do have an inflated sense of self, they also have a **disturbed identity**. In other words, because their sense of self is exaggerated, it is also rigid. There can never be room for changes because they like it just the way they are. For this reason, their identity is fragile. The stability of their character depends on maintaining their image.

When identities are fluid, they can accommodate various characteristics depending on the situation. For example, if you are having an argument with someone and you say something offensive, you might feel guilty about your words. You then swallow your pride and apologize to the person or at least try to make amends. That level of fluidity—being able to switch from being stubborn in your arguments to concerning—allows you to improve yourself. In the case of narcissists, don't expect anything to change. At least, not easily.

Since they have a rigid system of traits, it also becomes difficult for them to **rely** on others. They would never ask for help, even when they desperately need it. Doing so would make them think that someone else is better than them. That is something they would never admit to.

But what happens when this identity is not given the emotional, mental, or perhaps even physical sustenance that it so craves? In that case, the narcissist becomes **bored** and experiences a sense of **emptiness**. Often, they become restless and, in some cases, depressed. When such negative emotions manifest inside them, they look for ways to change their situation. They might manipulate others by using guilt or blame, trying to make someone else responsible for what they are going through.

Because they only see things from a monochromatic perspective, where something is either the way they want it or not, they are unable to make **successful life transitions**. They do not like altering their professional goals to improve their lives. They even try to avoid realistic aims in both their professional and personal lives. Any compromises that are required by work, school, and relationships might feel intolerable to the narcissist. When it comes to young adults, they "fail to launch" into their lives. In other words, they cannot keep a job, maintain a relationship, or learn a skill long enough to see positive progress.

It isn't all bad, however. Despite the various negative qualities of narcissism, there is a flip side to it as well. Being a narcissist has its benefits. The caveat is that you should have healthy doses of narcissism. If you are on an extreme end, then you might only exercise the dangerous qualities of narcissism.

So, what are these good qualities of narcissism?

According to researchers from Queen's University Belfast, a healthy dose of narcissism leads to a **tough mind** (Papageorgiou et al., 2018). Being emotionally tough is a valuable trait. It allows you to avoid sensitive attacks, face life's challenges head-on, and have the determination to see things through. You tend to be ambitious and put in the effort to gain rewards, whether in the professional or personal sphere.

With a safe level of narcissism, you might also be **fairly assertive**. You might wonder how that could be beneficial. The truth is that in life, you need to balance empathy and assertiveness since you might need to employ either trait depending on the situation. You cannot always be nice to everyone. Sometimes, you need to assert your points, ideas, requests, and answers. Otherwise, people may not take you seriously and could walk all over you. If that happens, then things could get dangerous. I am talking NPD-level dangerous.

Narcissists are always looking for potential victims, and when they find someone who does not stand firm on their points and ideas, it is as though they have found a secret stash of treasure they can't wait to get their hands on.

When you have safe levels of narcissism, you have **confidence**, but you also have **awareness**. Having dangerous levels of narcissism means that people don't want to evaluate their levels of confidence; they are simply the best at everything. However, a healthy dose of narcissism allows you to know the difference between confidence and arrogance. You know your shortcomings and understand the strengths you can exploit. You understand that you are not perfect, and that is alright with you. Your main goal is to improve. There is a certain awareness where you understand that you are a learner.

Because of this confidence, you can get things done without bringing others down. You are also open to **collaborative work**. You are reciprocal, allowing yourself to enter into healthy relationships at work and in your personal life. People with extreme narcissism fall prey to the opinions and pressure of others easily. They react strongly to feedback. They cannot stand challenges. Healthy narcissism allows people to deal with peer pressure, outside opinions, and even the needs of others in a calm and collected manner.

As you are open to collaborative work and don't find pleasure in looking down on others, you also don't need anyone's **approval** to function. You know that to attain something or reach a level of success, a certain degree of effort is required. There are also chances that you might experience failure. Guess what? You are fine with that because you do things to accomplish your goals, not to gain the approval of others.

While on the path to success or achievement, you understand that things can happen when you are least prepared for them. You might experience wonderful success or disappointing failure. But you are okay with that. There is an understanding of how events occur beyond your control. Sometimes, circumstances halt your progress. Rather than have a rigid stance on life's challenges, you are **flexible**, more **fluid**. You roll with the changes, adapting to the scenarios.

In the end, because you are flexible, understand others, collaborate with people, and don't look down on someone, you have a great awareness of the concept of **respect**. You understand that people may have opinions and habits that are different from yours. That thought does not challenge you or make you feel inferior. You are comfortable agreeing to disagree. Respect for a person means you see the layer of human characteristics beneath all of the surface-level traits.

As you just saw, a healthy dose of narcissism does not harm anyone. We all crave attention, love, approval, understanding, and value. It is part of what makes us human beings. I work to achieve the love and respect of my children. I want them to know that I have been a terrific mother. Sure, people might show modesty about just how much approval or attention they might need. But deep down, they do want someone to show them they are loved, tell them they are wonderful, or treat them with kindness. Healthy narcissism allows you to look for those responses with confidence and without disrespecting anyone.

You're Not My Type

We know that there is a healthy form of narcissism and a toxic version. This stems from the idea that narcissism exists on a spectrum. It is also why we have different types of narcissism.

However, while we are on the subject of types, we have only discussed two so far. While these two are the more commonly used types of narcissism, it wouldn't be a spectrum if there weren't more.

Let me tell you, more there are indeed. Although in all fairness, I am making it out to seem as though there is a list of 10 different types of narcissism that we can explore. In reality, there are two more that we need to discuss.

If you perform a quick online search, you are bound to find different lists, each one claiming to have more than four types of narcissism. While I am not here to bash that information or claim that it is incorrect, I will say that people usually split the types of narcissism more times than is necessary. That is not wrong in and of itself since it gives a more varied view on the subject. You can distinguish more with more types. However, what you need to know are the four broad types.

You saw the grandiose (overt) and vulnerable (covert) types of narcissism. Here are the two you may not be aware of.

For the third type, we are looking at **communal narcissists**. From casual observations, communal narcissists seem to share similarities with their grandiose counterparts. They crave warmth, attention, and agreeableness from others. They don't want to stay in the shadows but want to be known by everyone as the best at something. The difference lies in *what* they want to be recognized for. While grandiose narcissists want to see themselves as the smartest, most talented, most charming, or most intelligent, communal narcissists want to be recognized as the kindest, most thoughtful, and most generous. They want people to look at them as though they are a saint with so much goodness in them that it is hard not to see them without imagining a light from heaven shining down on them.

Communal narcissists can appear forgiving and empathetic, but their selflessness is as selfish as the selfishness grandiose narcissists have. Their intention to do good does not stem from the need to do it but from a desire to gain power, a sense of entitlement, and low self-esteem. They know that the only way they can gain attention is by looking good-natured.

The fourth and final type is a malignant narcissist. As the name suggests, malignant narcissists can be quite dangerous. They are considered to be on the extreme end of the spectrum and are prone to violent and harmful displays of aggression and cruelty. They are the ones more likely to engage in physical abuse, sometimes even for trivial reasons. They take a twisted form of pleasure in wreaking havoc and destroying people's lives. In many cases, they just want to inflict chaos. That's it. Nothing else. Not for any particular reason. They just enjoy the suffering they cause.

However, despite everything I have just mentioned, do not mistake malignant narcissism for sociopathy. There is a difference between the two. A sociopath takes pleasure in harming someone, which sounds oddly similar to a malignant narcissist. However, a sociopath is mainly propelled to violence by their own self-interests. They don whatever persona is needed to achieve their goals. You could label them as con artists since they are not fixated on maintaining a certain image in front of others. They do what must be done to inflict pain and suffering.

In the case of malignant narcissists, their egos are at stake. They want to maintain an image in society. This image is a carefully crafted personality, and they know that they cannot inflict pain willy-nilly. After all, if they are careless about their actions, they might be found out, and that is something they don't want. As you can see, despite the lack of control over their emotions, malignant narcissists do possess some level of control, if only because it serves their own needs.

Once you have recognized the types, you also need to be aware of the idea that when narcissism reaches an extreme level, it might become a disorder. When that happens, we have narcissistic personality disorder on our hands.

In a Disorderly Fashion

There are a total of 10 different types of personality disorders, according to the American Psychiatric Association (What Are Personality Disorders?, 2013). Among them lies narcissistic personality disorder or NPD.

But before we delve into NPD in particular, let's try and understand just what a personality disorder is.

These days, it seems as though some people would like nothing better than to lump others into one disorder or another. That right there is a dangerous diagnosis to make. Disorders are extreme psychological conditions that are diagnosed by professionals using certain criteria. Each person's mental health is unique. So, while there are certain guidelines that psychologists use, it eventually boils down to understanding the individual's psychological makeup to arrive at an accurate conclusion. It is for this reason that psychologists prefer a one-on-one with the patient. They don't want to make guesses based on outside suggestions and information. What they want to do is personally evaluate the individual.

Regardless, here are the patterns of behavior that guide a personality disorder. Do note that if a person satisfies only one of these psychological conditions, there is a minute chance that they have a disorder. For anyone to have a personality disorder, at least two of the below criteria should be met.

The way a person thinks about themself and others around them. If a person is critical of their own personality but kind to others, then they might have a case of low self-esteem. It does not mean that they have a disorder. However, if someone were to consider themselves superior to others, then the intensity of their thinking—coupled with other criteria on this list—decides what disorder they may have and how severe it is.

Their emotional responses. Are they quick to anger? Do they feel frustrated with even trivial matters? How do they respond when someone is in the spotlight? How much envy do they carry when they see someone boast about themselves? All of these factors, plus a lot more, help in finding out just what disorder the person might have.

The way they relate to people. We are talking about empathy. However, sometimes, we may find ourselves in a position where we may not be able to empathize with someone because we haven't gone through the same experiences they have. In such cases, we do try to find points to relate to, which leads to a certain understanding of the other's situation.

Control over one's behavior. This includes the way people behave in front of one person or a crowd. Are they quick to make a scene? Do they humiliate others easily? Are they always trying to gain attention?

Using the above criteria, let us look at NPD. Let's take the second point, which highlights emotional responses. People with NPD are prone to angry outbursts, especially when their status is challenged or their ideas questioned. Alternatively, they might become impatient and be unable to hold themselves back from showing their impatience.

Let us take another example and find out how it relates to NPD. Criteria number three talks about how a person can relate to someone else. In the case of a narcissist, they don't even attempt to try and understand someone. As long as they receive what they want, they don't care about anyone else.

If you look at the other criteria, then you might be able to use them to discover narcissistic traits in an individual and confirm whether they are likely to have NPD or not. However, there are a few more essential points you have to keep in mind:

- "Likely to have" does not mean that "they definitely have." If you find out that your friend has dangerous levels of narcissism, or might have NPD, then your first course of action is to find out how you have been affected. Then slowly give yourself more and more space. We are going to talk about self-defense (I'm not talking about boxing or Muay Thai) and other techniques that you can apply in your life to protect yourself from your friend in chapters 4 and 5.
- You might hear people casually throw around the term NPD, but the disorder is not as common as you might think. Only about 1% of the general population has NPD.

- The disorder cannot be diagnosed from a distance. If you feel that your friend might have NPD, ask them to visit a therapist and receive a professional evaluation. This might also help them find ways to improve their lives.
- Finally, remember that just because someone has NPD does not make them dangerous. The disorder itself can be an indication of mental illness and should not be considered a moral failing.

All of this might seem fairly confusing, especially when you are wondering just how narcissism can be different from NPD. Even narcissists are capable of harm, so why can't they all be grouped under the same umbrella term? As I have mentioned a few times before, it is not easy to attach a disorder to someone. While it might seem as though you are experiencing emotional and mental fatigue, it might just be because your friend is a narcissist in its distilled form. But what does that mean really? "Distilled form"? Is there a "complex form" as well?

To answer the questions above, we need to understand how narcissism differs from NPD. The human experience of needing attention, admiration, and love is normal. There is no other way to put it, but that need in itself is a form of narcissism. Sometimes, people have more of that need. For whatever reason, they feel dissatisfied with what they have and they crave copious amounts of what they receive emotionally. However, they are still able to function normally in many ways.

My husband was manipulative. He could never see himself as wrong and tried so hard to put himself at the center of our lives and practically pushed me to the sidelines. After much work, he began to slowly curb his narcissism. He began to apologize for the wrongs that he did. It might be fairly difficult, but narcissists can see the error of their ways and are capable of changing their personalities by themselves.

On the other hand, those with NPD cannot see the error of their ways. It's like dialing up every trait of a narcissist to the extreme. At this point, they need intervention and professional help. You cannot change them through mere conversations. Even though it might seem as though they are responding to you, in reality, they are merely biding their time to strike back at you.

I once knew somebody who had NPD, yet they would never admit to themselves that anything was wrong with them. All of the narcissistic traits were so ingrained in their psyche that they would employ them unconsciously. For example, the person would automatically resort to a lie before speaking the truth. It didn't matter if the question asked was trivial. They would simply choose to tell a fabricated tale.

During one of our meetings at a cafe, they had forgotten to place the order for a particular drink. Rather than admit that it had slipped their mind, they created an elaborate tale of why the drink order wasn't placed. They talked about already ordering it but blamed the barista for not listening to their order properly. They even blamed the music from the speakers above, claiming that perhaps the high volume might have been the reason for the barista's error. All of a sudden, they shifted the blame from them to someone else. At that point, I knew I couldn't confront them about it since they could have had a violent reaction.

My husband had committed a similar lie, except this time it was at the cinemas and concerned the tickets. He had forgotten to get the seats that we had discussed. When asked, he instantly blamed the staff. However, when I mentioned that he made the mistake himself and it was okay to admit it, he changed his stance. No longer did the lying narcissist exist. In its place was a human guilty of something he had done. I knew from the look on his face that he wasn't particularly sorry about his mistake but was instead sorry about the lie he had immediately conjured. That was fine. I didn't care about the tickets anyway. I just didn't want my husband to lie to the one person who had stuck by him through the highs and lows.

Narcissists can have a normal life. Anyone with NPD, on the other hand, forces their personality as the new normal. Even if you act as a mirror for their words and actions, you won't change their mind easily. Rather than feel guilty, they might immediately take up a defensive stance and slowly plot your demise in their minds. Yes, they can carry a grudge for as long as it takes to exact some form of revenge on you.

I have known people with NPD to go so far as to use vengeance and take every opportunity they have to torment the victim. They do this even if the reason itself was trivial. You might be in a group of people. Each person might be poking fun at someone else.

You, being a good sport, laugh at the jokes thrown at you. It's harmless fun, and nobody is taking it seriously. But little would you expect there to be a wolf among the sheep. The wolf is the narcissist (remember, they have NPD). You decide—hey, everyone is having fun, right?—to poke fun at the narcissist.

You are in for a world of discomfort.

NPD Sociopath? Sociocist? Narcipath? Socionarcipath?

There exists a big difference between someone with NPD and someone with sociopathy. Where a narcissist has a certain worldview that they adhere to, a sociopath is flexible. You can find a sociopath responding with compassion to a loved one's loss, cheering the accomplishment of a colleague, or sharing a genuine moment of joviality with family members. They can blend into situations seamlessly. There is no easy way to spot them unless they happen to make a mistake that you catch. A narcissist has a carefully constructed persona. They might feel annoyed when things don't go their way, become clueless as to how to react to novel situations, and sometimes be unresponsive.

Not a sociopath. They are not deterred by new situations. One could say that they revel in the knowledge that they might have a new conquest.

But Is There Such a Thing as a Narcissistic Sociopath?

There is. Before we delve into that, let me offer this guideline. Any sociopath can be a narcissist, but not any narcissist can be a sociopath. When someone uses the term narcissistic sociopath, they are not referring to someone with NPD who has a conscience so cold it feels like a mythological hell. What they are referring to is a sociopath who is vain, conscious about their self-image, and takes offense at the slightest comment.

The biggest difference lies in their intentions. Sociopaths enjoy the thrill of manipulating someone to inflict the maximum damage in their lives. They live for the chaos and, in some cases, the violence. On the other hand, a narcissistic sociopath manipulates others to get ahead in their lives. They do take thrill in the pain they inflict, but they are also focused on how others reflect on themselves.

A person might have a close friend who is a narcissistic sociopath. The sociopath might show attention and compassion to such a degree that the person is unaware of the nefarious intentions hidden behind the smiles. What is their goal? Perhaps the person might have another friend. This second friend could be wealthy. They might be influential. They could be smarter, good-looking, successful, or hold a lot of accomplishments. They might have something that the narcissistic sociopath might need. For that reason, they use the first friend for their own needs. They manipulate, lie, and deceive because, in the end, they will discard the first friend when they are close to the second friend. But that's not all they will do. Along the way, they will cause as much destruction in the person's life as possible. The more painful the results, the more glee and joy they experience.

A narcissist might have a limit, but a sociopath is unhinged. It is like an eagle honing in on prey. The bird won't simply stop before it sinks its claws into the poor animal, congratulating itself on a wonderful scare tactic. It will go in for the attack. That is how a sociopath thinks. They don't stop at the last moment just because they have received what they wanted.

A Mind of Their Own

No matter what type of narcissist you are referring to, there is a depth of knowledge as to why they behave the way they do. I suppose talking about the types of narcissists and the reasons they have become what they have is quite important. However, it is also vital to understand how their minds work. For it is within their mental domain that we shall unlock the mysteries of who they really are. Think of it as looking at a watch and knowing what it does and why it performs in a certain way. But to know 'how' means you have to open it and take a peek at its mechanisms. We are going to do the same—minus opening up anyone to take a peek inside since that would be quite bizarre and horrific, I would imagine—with a narcissist.

We shall take a peek into their minds.

Chapter 3:

How Narcissists Think

I am a person deserving of love and kindness.

Adrian (named changed for privacy concerns) was a narcissist. He was also someone I was helping to overcome his condition. He genuinely wanted to change. When I asked him about his actions, he would admit that he had wronged many people in his life just so he could gain an advantage. Most striking was the first conversation I had with him.

I can still recollect the day. A young man in his late twenties stopped by my place of private practice. I am not a psychiatrist, mind you, but he was related to a friend of mine, and she had asked me to help him in his situation. I couldn't exactly deny her request, and neither could I invite people over to my house. It wasn't because I was threatened by him. Rather, I think I like to keep my personal life away from any other work I do. My home is my sanctuary, even though it hadn't been for a while. Plus, I wasn't about to bring any other narcissist into my home where my sons also lived. They didn't need to be in the presence of more than one narcissist.

Adrian was sporting a plaid shirt and blue jeans. There was an air of confidence about him. But with my years of experience, I could see the real reason he was there seeking my consultation.

When he sat down in front of me, he seemed so sure of himself. One could imagine he was there to simply catch up with an old friend, not as a patient. I allowed him a moment to settle down. It wasn't that I was trying to make him feel uncomfortable. It also wasn't about power-play. I wanted him to understand the reason he was there sitting in front of me. Eventually, he made eye contact—briefly, I might add—before looking away outside the giant window. I admit that I had a beautiful view of the city, which was intentional. I had also placed my office on one of the top floors, allowing the viewer to feel as though they have a sense of elevation. They feel powerful, looking down on things. It's a little trick to settle people or my business clients down, especially when they become angsty or impatient.

After he had made eye contact and started looking out the window, I allowed Adrian another two minutes before speaking.

"Are you a narcissist, Adrian?" I asked.

He looked at me. This time, the eye contact was longer. Perhaps he was looking into me as much as I was trying to glimpse into his mind. That was okay. I had nothing to hide. I truly wanted to know.

I had to believe that he might have seen the professional curiosity in my eyes. He nodded. "Yeah," he answered. The nonchalance hadn't left him. "That's what everyone says anyway."

A partial admission. That was okay. I could see that he had admitted his shortcoming initially but had switched tactics. Perhaps he was too surprised by himself to admit it. Maybe he wasn't expecting the direct question, which might have taken him back so much that his mind must have blanked, leaving behind just the truth.

You might imagine that this phenomenon of narcissists admitting their traits is rare. On the contrary, studies have shown that with the two questionnaire types mentioned earlier (Narcissistic Personality Inventory [NPI] featuring 40 questions and the single-item questionnaire that only features one question), narcissists will not deny who they are (Psychology Today, 2019). Even more surprising is the fact that those who answer the single-item questionnaire score higher on the NPI than people who haven't answered the single-item questionnaire.

Strange, isn't it? It is as though narcissists want to be found out. While it is true that they would prefer to manipulate people from the shadows, there comes a time when they reach a level of success that they become proud of. When that happens, they want to let their accomplishments be known. After all, they feel as though they have reached the pinnacle of their achievements. However, it also boils down to something much simpler. No one has ever asked them if they are narcissists. They become so used to hiding that when confronted with a question about their identity, they don't know how to react. All they can do is just admit it.

It was the same with Adrian. He just couldn't wait to tell someone who he really was.

After talking to Adrian and many other narcissists throughout my studies, I began to see a few patterns that other professionals before me had noticed.

So, what motivates narcissists? What is the power that keeps their internal mechanisms running?

The image is one of perfection. This is probably the most obvious of all reasons, but it is one worth mentioning; they need to preserve a certain image. As mentioned earlier, narcissists create a version of themselves that they cultivate. This version is based on numerous factors. It could be based on past trauma, where they felt they were lacking something. For example, if they were bullied as children for their looks, then they might grow up fussing over little details of their appearance.

It could also be because of something that they witnessed. Perhaps it was a movie. It could be a magazine they were reading. Regardless of the source, they began to yearn for something they saw with an unhealthy obsession. Bear in mind that it is okay to be passionate about an accomplishment, even if you just want to get a physical item. However, what is not okay is when you begin to manipulate, harm, or destroy others to get what you want.

A lie is a better reality than the truth. They have to be right, even when they are wrong. Honesty does not have a presence in their beliefs. The Earth is flat, and that is the final word. I'm not saying all flat-Earthers are narcissists, but that is how a narcissist operates; they don't care about facts. Their lies build a world that they can dive into whenever they need affirmations or a quick boost of confidence.

They feel a constant sense of danger. What is that person trying to do? Why did they look at me that way? Is that the right way to say hello? Are they trying to prove that they are above me by opening the door for me?

There are so many thoughts that zip through a narcissist's mind, it is as though their thoughts are having a popularity contest to see who gets noticed. It gets worse. Most of those thoughts are trying to dissect the actions, words, expressions, emotions, ideas, and reactions of others, trying to find out the underlying wicked intentions of the person, even if such intentions don't exist at all. You could walk up to them in the middle of a street and wave hi. They might think you are just trying to show off your confidence. You could do just about anything, and it will never please the narcissist.

They have inconsistencies in their consistency. Mr. and Mrs. A were a couple who had approached me to find out about the presence of narcissism in the relationship. Each blamed the other for it. I decided to talk to them about it, taking time to understand each person's perspective without jumping to any conclusions.

The more I listened to their stories, the more I realized the true depth of their situation. Mr. A had been receiving plenty of complaints and put-downs. In one instance, he had decided to help unload some of the work from his wife's shoulders by taking care of the dishes after he got home from work. She found his gesture insulting, blaming him for not trusting her to do the work. He was even accused of trying to make her feel guilty for keeping the dishes unwashed. Faced with the reaction from his wife, Mr. A stopped doing the dishes. Eventually, Mrs. A blamed him for placing all of the responsibilities on her. She would also mutter under her breath as she cleaned the dishes, and Mr. A caught phrases like "has no idea what I'm going through," "thinks I am one of those women who needs to live her life like a good housewife," and "why did he marry me if he simply wanted to boss me around?"

What Mrs. A truly wanted was not for her husband to wash the dishes or help her with chores. She wanted a sense of control. It made her feel powerful when her husband did exactly as she told him to. Eventually, her ideas turned the relationship toxic, even emotionally abusive.

Mrs. A's idea of controlling her husband was consistent. However, her approach to maintaining that idea was inconsistent. It could change, depending on the situation. That's how narcissists operate. As long as they have a certain goal to attain, they can change their approaches to fit the situation.

There is a lack of introspection. You might wonder how this point can exist, considering that narcissists are willing to admit who they are when faced with a direct question. The reality is that they know exactly who they are but don't allow it to surface. When one is manipulating someone, they are usually aware of their actions. When you are pleased with a performance or movie, you clap at the end because you want to. The act of manipulating is similar to clapping; people are aware of doing it. There are some rare situations where a child learns to adopt manipulative tendencies because they watch their parents or influential people do it all of the time. It becomes second nature.

Narcissists know that they are manipulating someone. They know their nature. However, they don't indulge in further introspection. Doing so would mean finding faults that they don't want to see. The more we delve into something, the more we see its flaws. Introspection is similar to a detailed examination, and it is capable of revealing our weaknesses. As we know by now, being weak is not what a narcissist wants to be.

They have to win at any cost. Typically, they make others pay the price for the challenges they face on the road to success.

I had an encounter with a certain young man. Let's call him Harold. He once had his sights set on a nice piece of computer hardware. Such was his desire to own the item that he borrowed money from his friends. Here is where things get interesting. He had cultivated such strong relationships with people that even after lending him money, sometimes when they could not afford to, they never asked him to pay them back. They were worried about hurting his feelings. Harold knew how they would react. He used his influence over their emotional attachment to make them do something for him.

The last I heard of Harold, his old friend circle had all but disappeared. He had borrowed one time too many and would always casually shrug off requests to return the money. He would act as though the idea of paying someone back wasn't important. There was even an instance when he began to tear up, making up grand tragedies about his life. The emotional and mental exhaustion got to his friends, and they could not bear to have his presence in their lives.

Narcissists do not care how they reach their goals. They won't even put in the effort themselves if they can avoid it (which they typically try to do).

Command and Control

So, why manipulate? Why do they want people to do as they command? What is the purpose of having so much control over someone? Is it just to achieve a set goal?

Not really. There are several reasons why narcissists choose to manipulate.

They just don't like being **confronted**. Manipulation can be a defensive move as much as an offensive plan. When narcissists know that someone is about to corner them about their words or actions, they manipulate their way out of the situation.

It does not even have to be a situation where they are on the **defensive**. Sometimes, manipulation can be used to put the ball in your court. Usually, your intention might be to have a conversation with the narcissist. You might not be expecting an attack from the narcissist, but an attack they might deliver. Even if you were prepared for an offense, you might not expect the kind of verbal harm they might throw your way. They could bring up any topic. They might even twist the truth. Even if you had mentally prepared yourself, there are moments when you might be compelled to say something to avoid the ghastly things they are capable of saying.

Doubt shatters confidence. It can destroy beliefs. Doubt is exactly what the narcissist wants to plant in your head. They know that when you begin to have second thoughts about what you initially wanted to speak about or convey, then they escape from a confrontation or, worse, turn the tables around so you look like the guilty party.

Sometimes, it does not even have to do with being offensive, defensive, or just sowing the seeds of doubt. Sometimes, it just so happens that the narcissist is trying to mask their **aggression**. Deep down, there may be a metaphorical cauldron of rage bubbling. It cannot wait to erupt. But for whatever reason—maybe you are in a public place or perhaps the narcissist does not have enough ammunition against you—the narcissist refuses to engage with you. Instead, they hide their true feelings through duplicitous words.

Other times, they simply want to avoid **responsibility**. Life is a challenging ride, and quite often, you need to take charge of things. That means you have to face the ups and downs of your decision. You might have to put in the effort to reap the rewards of your actions. A narcissist prefers the easy way. When responsibility seeks them, they manipulate people to avoid it.

When it does not concern responsibility, it might just concern **change**. We saw how narcissists love consistency. Sure, they might be forced to approach situations from a different perspective, but their eventual goal is to get things back to the way they were.

Voicing Out

There is one more factor that we can use to find out how narcissists function. That factor is a voice.

It isn't just any voice. You have it. I do. So does everyone else in the world. The degree of intensity of the voice varies from person to person. Your life experiences, personal relationships, childhood, environment, and interactions come together to create this voice.

We are talking about the critical inner voice.

Everyone's critical inner voice is essentially a string of negative attitudes and thoughts about themselves and the people they know. It is a crucial component of maladaptive behaviors, which are behaviors that intentionally impede someone's ability to learn about novel situations or react to challenging circumstances. The strength of the inner critical voice decides just how much progress a person might be able to make in life.

The voice is mainly defensive. It is cynical about a lot of factors, even when there are many things you can be thankful for. It has a hostile disposition, mainly targeting you. When the voice speaks, it does not just have feedback about beliefs, ideas, and memories; it can also evoke emotions such as shame, envy, sadness, anger, and other emotions that can prove to be mentally debilitating.

It is the voice that tells you that you are worthless. It is the voice that convinces you that you are never going to be anything better than you are. You may hear it during moments of lengthy procrastination, telling you to just give up on doing something since it does not matter in real life. In fact, one of the reasons you procrastinate is because of this voice. When faced with a challenge, the balance between the extent of the problem and the number of solutions you have shifts in favor of the problems. You begin to see life's challenges as insurmountable objects. There is a voice whispering to you, sometimes unbeknownst to your conscious mind, that no matter what you do, you are never going to overcome the challenge. Might as well sit down, order a pizza, and boot up Netflix. *Tiger King* is on. Or *The Witcher.* Your pick.

It is also the voice that tells you to take your own life.

According to research published by psychologists from the American Psychological Association (Firestone, 2006), the critical inner voice is responsible for suicides and suicide attempts. The psychologists suggested trying to calm this voice in therapy so that patients could better analyze their surroundings and have the ability to rationally explore solutions.

You really cannot escape the voice easily. After all, you can't stop your mind functioning with just the snap of your fingers. You probably shouldn't either since I would imagine that could be dangerous. Imagine making your mind disappear. How, then, would you *think* to make it reappear? That's a deep question, but it is not the focus of this book.

In most people, the critical inner voice is a self-destructive mechanism. People find that their minds are attacking themselves. However, in the case of a narcissist, the critical inner voice mainly targets others. After all, in their eyes, they are perfect and can do no wrong.

When the inner voice strikes, it aims to bring down others for the benefit of the narcissist.

If a friend or someone close to the narcissist receives praise, then the narcissist might think: *I could have done that. He was lucky he was there at the right time and the right place.*

When it is a family member's birthday: *Come on. Really? When was the last time you twats ever thought of me?*

They have this black-and-white idea that if they aren't great, they aren't important, so they constantly bring others down to boost their own sense of self.

But an inner voice doesn't come from nowhere. It relies on you to feed it. Think of a seed. You plant the seed, water it, give it sufficient sunlight, and watch it grow into a plant. You can easily destroy this life since the plant isn't strong enough to withstand the power of your hands. Eventually, the plant grows into a small tree. You can still take it down, but you might need sharp tools for the job. Your hands may not be enough unless you have been bench-pressing 100 pounds as though you were lifting shopping bags. Eventually, that seed is now a large tree and no amount of gym workout is going to give you the power to pull it down. You might need a powerful tool, like a chainsaw. Even then, the work involved in bringing down the tree and disposing of it isn't easy.

Your inner voice is that seed. You might be able to try and curb its growth in the initial stages, but once it feeds on your fears, anger, frustrations, envy, disgust, and sadness, it grows into something strong. It takes root deep within your consciousness.

That's when things get complicated.

Optimus Prime!

Do you know what priming is?

I think it is best to explain the concept with an example. Picture yourself heading home or someplace you visit regularly (your job, the path you take to jog every day, or the way to your parent's house). You begin your journey fully aware of the destination. Along the way, you see a cat. The sight sparks a memory of the one time you saw a beautiful tabby at your friend's place. Such a furry cat. You wish you had it! Speaking of animals, wasn't there recent news about scientists trying to argue that dolphins need to have human rights (BBC, 2012)? Thoughts about dolphins take you to your plan to buy a small aquarium at home, which then moves on to the idea of seafood, which then takes you to—

Whoa! Wait just a moment! You have reached your destination. That's odd. You don't quite remember all the details of your trip. You might remember the occasional glimpses of people and objects, but the entire journey is foggy, as though your mind just took the movie of your life and decided to edit out some parts just because it felt like it.

In reality, what you experienced was a psychological phenomenon called highway hypnosis. Because you were so used to traveling the route over and over again, your mind put that part of the journey into automation. In other words, your subconscious mind took over. It's like mental cruise control with your consciousness left to ponder dolphins, cats, the ending of *Inception*, if chickens are dinosaurs or if dinosaurs are chickens, and your last double-espresso mochaccino.

Keep that in mind; your subconscious sometimes puts things on autopilot that you do repeatedly. It is why basketball players practice rigorously. They want to get used to the motions of passing, shooting, and dribbling so that when they play, they can focus on other important elements of the court, such as opponents and teammate position, gaps, and other strategies. Imagine paying so much attention to every action. That would be fairly stressful and distracting to the basketball players. In fact, think about your own life. Most of what you do is automatic. When you walk, you don't constantly pay attention to your feet. Your breathing, some of the words you use as a response (such as involuntarily saying "thank you"), blinking, and other small actions are automatic because you have done them so many times before.

This sense of automation also happens to thoughts. The way you behave right now is because of ideas, actions, and behaviors that you have cultivated over time. You employ these ideas over and over again. Think of the next time someone takes a pass in front of your car. Your immediate reaction might be one of frustration. But have you ever wondered why that happens? It is as though it was automatic. You feeling compelled to drop a coin into the cup of a homeless person, your preference for a certain type of dessert, and your favorite color are all ingrained in your mind. Without knowing, you might pick the blue paint for your home because you like it. You don't ask yourself why you like it. You just do. Because the reasons don't matter. Your subconscious has already stored your likes, dislikes, fears, hopes, dreams, desires, and plans in its vast repository.

In many ways, your subconscious mind is a truly powerful force able to control your emotions and, therefore, your actions and decisions as well. That, right there, is priming.

When a stimulus (and by that, I mean emotion, memory, idea, or experience) from the past affects the way you think, act, speak, and feel in the present, then the phenomenon is called priming.

The same level of automation happens in a narcissist's mind. They have trained their minds to think only about themselves. They have frequently scorned others. That idea of extreme focus on self-interest takes root in their subconscious, eventually growing into something gnarled and disfigured. Their subconscious primes them to manipulate others to get what they want because that is one of the few ways they like to approach situations.

Narcissists automatically envy others, despise them, attempt to control them, create a scene, think only about themselves, and perform various actions related to narcissism. If you were to see someone fall, you might cry out in shock or leap to your feet to help them. You do it without thinking. If a narcissist spots someone fall, thoughts of "they deserve it," "what a loser," or "I'm not getting up to help that idiot" flash through their mind.

Sword and Shield

A narcissist's primes are their sword. They apply it in nearly every situation. Remember Adrian? When he first entered my office, he started forming ideas about me. He thought I was a pretentious psychologist without the faintest idea of what I was doing. In fact, he thought that I was an "old hack."

How do I know all of this? He told me eventually as I got to know more about him and he became comfortable speaking his mind.

We talked about the sword. What about the shield?

Once again, it is their primes.

They have created this idea deep in their subconscious that they have to think about themselves in most scenarios. For this reason, their mind automatically goes on the defensive when they perceive a threat or are anticipating one. They have strong personalities not because they feel confident but because they are extremely vulnerable and are preparing themselves to reject any feedback, criticism, or form of communication that they don't like. They are so fragile that anyone who questions or criticizes them is perceived as a threat, and they must respond accordingly.

Because their personality is also covered in a facade and they feel so alienated and empty, they don't have any real purpose in their lives. You might want to become successful in your job. They might want to be successful in theirs, not because they want it but simply because they think it might enhance their status. Eventually, they have a collection of wants and no real goals to help them.

Their lack of meaningful purpose results in them looking to their narcissistic tendencies for help. Their need to be dominant, bring down others, maintain a certain image, or destroy people's lives to get something they want becomes their goal. They constantly act on their impulses, which eventually become rooted in their subconscious.

They prime themselves to believe that the only way they can find true meaning in their lives is when they are being narcissists.

Chapter 4:

Dealing With a Narcissist

It's a touchdown. We have landed at our destination. This place is for all you survivors, victims, and sufferers. Before we reach the main sights and landmarks, let us take a moment to recognize something.

Heal Thyself

Before we can talk about the many ways you can deal with a narcissist, we need to first make sure that you are ready for the battles ahead. Yes, there are going to be numerous battles. Some, you might win. Others, you might lose. But that is normal. What you are going to do is find ways to tackle the narcissist in your life without losing yourself to their abuse and manipulations.

Baby Steps

You are going to learn the steps toward healing. Every victim's journey is unique. There are so many circumstances and narcissistic characteristics that it is clear a one-size-fits-all approach is not going to work. However, what we can look at are a number of options that you can apply to your life. You can choose one option, or you can choose all of them.

I recommend that you go through each step since they will help you gain a sense of control over your life, bring a level of peace that you might need, and allow you to reflect on yourself. Introspection is beneficial on your part since you can examine the damage you have suffered and find out how you have been acting in the presence of the narcissist.

So, here are the 10 steps to healing.

Step 1: Understand the characteristics of narcissists present in this book. Apply them to the friends in your life. Recognize those habits that are abusive and pathological. Stop giving any excuses for your friend's actions, and examine each action without judgment to see the impact it has on your life.

Has your friend been trying to prevent you from meeting other people? Are they constantly checking up on you and expecting you to let them know your whereabouts? Have they tried to accuse your family or colleagues of something nefarious without actual evidence? Were there signs that your friend was capable of resorting to physical violence, but they brought themselves under control? Think carefully and analyze rationally. Most importantly, think about your friend's words, actions, and emotions and how they impacted you. This brings us to the next step.

Step 2: Stop trying to empathize with the narcissist. Do not project your sense of morality on them. At this point, you matter. If you start concerning yourself with the narcissist, then you might accidentally shrug off a casual remark, action, or reaction that could otherwise be construed as abusive. I want you to say this, "Right now, I matter." Since you matter, your reality matters as well, which takes us to the next step.

Step 3: Start affirming your reality. I want you to read that first line again, but this time, emphasize the word 'your.' Stop validating the reality that the narcissist has created for you. Don't believe the distortions the abuser has placed in your life.

For example, have they recently been trying to convince you that your parents don't have your best interests at heart and that perhaps you should just leave home? I don't want you to deny or accept their idea. Rather, use your own experience—after all, you know your parents best—to try and see if they have been trying to stop you from achieving your goals in life. Don't jump to conclusions quickly. Perhaps your parents have been telling you to avoid traveling to a country for your vacation not because they are trying to control your life but because they are worried about your safety. If that is the case, then have a conversation with them about it. Take your time to analyze your life from a fresh and singular perspective, yours.

Step 4: One of the best ways to affirm your reality is by building social links. Create more relationships. Find people who have your best interests at heart. Reconnect with those you had lost touch with because of the narcissist. The more people you have, the more they can help you stay accountable for your reality. That way, if you start to act in a way that does not reflect your personality, they can let you know.

Step 5: Adopt self-care methods such as meditation, physical exercise, or even hobbies to amplify the effects of the healing process. The more you take care of yourself, the better you can flush the presence of the narcissist from your life.

Step 6: You need to create a "reverse script" to counteract the effects of the narcissist's words. Think of this step as a reverse UNO card; you are responding to narcissistic influence with your own remarks. You take the ideas the narcissist has written for you and then slowly add in your ideas as a response. If they had told you how lazy you had been, even when it wasn't true, then your reverse script should include the times you worked hard to achieve what you wanted. You can even write down the reverse script so that you can use it as a reference whenever you need it.

Step 7: Maintaining little to no contact with the narcissist during the healing phase. You don't want them trying to interrupt the process. They might plant dangerous ideas in your mind, rendering all the effort you had made so far in your healing process a waste.

Step 8: If you picked up any self-sabotaging behaviors or addictions when you were with your friend, then make sure that you give attention to them. Find ways to slowly rid them from your life. If you followed Step 4, then you should also be able to perform this step in the presence of people who support you and love you for who you are. The presence of genuine care can be a transformative experience.

Step 9: Start looking at the many ways in which you have made positive contributions to people's lives, work, and society at large. Have you been killing it at the office? Start thinking about that in detail. Do you enjoy making your nieces and nephews smile? Think about that in great detail. It is time to start overwriting all the negative ideas the narcissist created about you with positive notions about yourself.

Step 10: Finally, it is time to align your focus with the goals, purposes, hobbies, and interests you had originally had before you met the narcissist. Don't have a goal? Don't worry. You now have the freedom to think about what you want to do. Planning to get a promotion at work? Maybe that holiday that you always wanted to take? Spend more time with family? Start your business? Binge-watch *Lord of the Rings*? It is up to you. Do what makes you happy. Reconnect with your goals. Bring back the joy in your life.

Peace Offering

Perhaps you have a friend you have known for a long time. You may not be able to escape their presence all the time. There are going to be instances when you might have to be with them. Or maybe you have a colleague whom you cannot simply get rid of because you need to work with them to accomplish your tasks.

What do you do in such scenarios? How do you get your point across effectively?

Firstly, let them **have the spotlight**. In fact, hand it over to them. If you are ever going to receive a chance of getting your point across, start by admiring them. Listen to them boast about their achievements. Praise their toys or their ego. You need a lot of effort to accomplish this feat. Narcissists are practically begging for people to throw appreciation their way. Sometimes, they might even find a way to congratulate themselves. Let them. Pretend that they are saying something interesting just so they can give you the chance to finish your task. Be careful, however. If they start placing demands or exercising their will over you, be firm and reject them. Don't create an opening where you fall under their control.

When dealing with them, make sure that you get whatever **you want from them first**. The reason for this is that if you let them have their way first, then they are probably going to keep you there for a while. Once you have completed your task, take a moment to allow them to brag about themselves. Then excuse yourself from the conversation.

If the narcissist constantly attacks you or harms you emotionally, then try to turn the tables on them. **Put them in the spotlight**, and let them know that their actions or words are harming you.

If you have been showing them compassion, then you need to **stop doing that**. They take advantage of your good nature to try and attack you more. In fact, many narcissists are aware that you might not be able to keep your tough exterior active for too long since your kindness might eventually show. They wait for that moment, ready to pounce on the opportunity to take advantage of you.

If the narcissist is getting in your way too often, then your best strategy is to **avoid them** for a while. You can do this until you have finished your tasks and done what you want to do. After that, you can perhaps admire them for a little while to stroke their ego. Don't try to provoke them in any manner. They are known to hold grudges for a long time, and you don't want to constantly worry about a narcissist's attack.

Try to put their actions into a **broader context**. Ask them what other people would think of their actions if word got out about what they did. When they know that there is a chance that their reputation might be tarnished, they will tone down their behavior. Make sure that you don't speak in anger, or it might come out as a threat. That might trigger a narcissist's defense mechanisms. Rather, show your disappointment in their actions.

You could use a personal analogy. For example, you can say that their actions would never be accepted by anyone in your community, friend circle, or family. What you are doing is letting them know that you are not alone. You have people you trust, and they won't be pleased with the narcissist's actions.

Finally, you can **restrict the narcissist's involvement** in your life to certain areas. For example, if you are dealing with a colleague, then you don't have to spend time with them outside work hours. Only reach out to them when both of your tasks intersect. If it is your friend, then feel free to reject their suggestions for spending time with them unless you have another friend with you.

Mounting an Attack

Narcissists are not fair fighters. They don't follow any rules as long as they gain an advantage. I have come across people who are unable to vocalize what they experienced with their abuser. They don't know how to explain the kind of attacks they face. The narcissist can use sympathy, anger, affection, and guilt within a short space of time. It is disorienting to the victim.

What you need to do is understand the emotional language of the narcissist. Use the information provided in this book about narcissists to keep a close eye on their behavior.

In a fight or confrontation, all narcissists are capable of seeing are their own anger and frustration. They are the ones who are hurt. They are the victims. That is a stance they will hold stubbornly. You have no chance of trying to make them see the error of their ways when they are in such a state of rage or hostility.

There are many tactics narcissists use to attack you, and they can broadly be categorized as direct and indirect attacks. Direct attacks include rage-induced speeches, where they try to put the blame on you and show how you are the true abuser, or insults and slurs that target your personality, race, background, or any other advantage they can get.

Indirect attacks can be in the form of silent treatment. Narcissists are known to ignore their victims for hours on end. They might frequently show frustration at something to point out the mistakes of the victim. They will try to act as though the victim is responsible for everything that is happening to them. Other tactics include spreading false information about the victim to someone else, sabotaging work, or transferring blame for a mistake that they made.

Dismantling the Narcissist

Firstly, remove all concepts of right or wrong. They are not going to admit to anything. You might have better success breaking a brick wall with your head than trying to make them confess. Don't try to find the fault. Rather, think about logically coming to a resolution. Find an answer that does not involve attacking the narcissist.

While you attempt to find a resolution, know that the narcissist might attempt to throw you off-guard or attack you. Do not let their words offend you.

In fact, they might try every way possible to distract you from your real purpose. They might even resort to lies. Whether they are talking about something that you did in the past, a personality quirk of yours, or a piece of information that they might have made up on the spot, they are going to use lies to evoke some response from you. Stay on track. Don't give them the satisfaction of knowing they have won.

Remember, you have a secret weapon that destroys a lie. This secret weapon is the truth. It does not matter whether they are confronting you directly or using other tricks to control you. Give them a dose of the truth medicine. For example, if a colleague is constantly trying to interrupt your work, criticizing your actions, or belittling you, then simply choose a direct approach. Ask them, "You seem oddly concerned with my work. Is there something on your mind? What you are doing is really distracting."

However, there might be moments where you are backed into a corner. Rather than confronting them aggressively, consider using another tactic, empathy. Let them know that you understand them. Show them that you care. Talk to them about how your actions might have hurt them, and assure them that you did not mean to cause them any discomfort. This might sound like you are admitting defeat, but know that you are merely trying to get yourself out of a sticky situation.

Remember that no matter what approach you use, try to use 'we' language. Don't alienate the narcissist by using statements starting with 'I' or 'you.' For example, instead of saying something like, "You should work on making this better," try saying something like, "We should work together to make this better." Don't try to talk about yourself to avoid blame. For example, don't say, "I wasn't the one who started this. You did this." Instead, you could say, "I know that we both would never want to bring this situation to where it is now."

You are trying to let the narcissist know that you want to work together with them to resolve the issue. Moreover, by not alienating them, you are not giving them opportunities to become defensive.

It isn't just the use of the 'we' language you should be aware of. You should also realize that your goal is to come to an amicable agreement if not a full resolution. More importantly, do not look for an apology. You are not going to get one. Even if you feel that the narcissist should apologize for what they did, don't act on those thoughts. It is a bitter pill to swallow, and you might feel as though the narcissist is getting away with what they have done. However, you might just avoid an even bigger incident in the future if you focus on avoiding blame.

When you are in those situations where it seems as though a confrontation is about to start, think about ways you can distract the narcissist. Use their tactics against them. It's like dangling a toy in front of a child, and many narcissists are like overgrown children who are not able to control their emotional impulses. Talk about the things that they like. Change the topic to focus on their interests.

Of course, this tactic might not be effective when you are in the middle of a confrontation. But it is effective to stop a confrontation or calm down the narcissist after fighting with them. Alternatively, you could ask the narcissist for a solution. While it might not resolve the situation, you might just make them feel superior. That is a way to distract them long enough for you to figure out your next course of action.

On the other hand, if you are not planning to avoid distracting the narcissist and instead are going to have a conversation, then there are a few points to remember:

- Make sure that you admit your mistakes. The way to an honest conversation is to show the narcissist that you are willing to admit that you might have done something wrong. Of course, if you were not at fault for anything, then don't invent a reason to be guilty.

- Talk about those moments when the narcissist displayed good qualities. Maybe they were understanding. Perhaps they were patient. Bring up those instances, and let the narcissist know that they don't always have to resort to negative behavior to resolve a conflict. Reach out to the goodness they might harbor in their minds. Additionally, know that narcissists are gluttons for positive feedback. Might as well give it to them.

- Even if you are tempted to, do not display negative reactions toward them. They might just use that as an excuse to blame you for the problem. What's worse, they might hold your reaction over you for as long as they want.

- No matter what direction the conversation takes, do not resort to ultimatums to conclude the issue. If you feel exhausted with the conversation, then forget about trying to end it quickly. Take a break. Let the narcissist know that you and they will continue the conversation later. Let them know that you need time to think. But do not let them know that you are exhausted. They might use it against you in future conversations to exhaust you, especially when things are not going their way. Another drawback to using ultimatums is that you might become as toxic as the narcissist. Do not stoop to their level.

- Remember that a narcissist's emotions are their own. Don't try to imagine that you caused their sadness, anger, or pain. As soon as you think that way, you might accidentally let the idea slip, and the narcissist will simply run with that. They might then keep blaming you for their emotions, knowing that you are probably doing the same. They are responsible for their reactions and emotions. If they are upset, it isn't because of you. It is simply because they want to be upset. Nothing more.

- Do not fight back with the narcissist. They might lure you into a conflict, and if you enter it, things might not go the way you want them to. The narcissist might suddenly shift stances. Or by seeing you engage in conflict, they might play the victim card by letting you know that you are hurting them. All of a sudden, you have become the abuser. If you feel yourself wanting to give the narcissist a piece of your mind, step away from the conversation. Take a break. It doesn't matter if you need an entire day to calm down; take it.

- Do not respond to the emotions bubbling in the room. This might be difficult if you are an empath or sensitive. For that reason, I recommend trying to set up a meeting in a public place. Perhaps a cafe with a cozy atmosphere might help you. However, if you think that the conversation might get heated, then it is best to not choose a public place for the meeting. Alternatively, you could create a positive mood for yourself. Before your conversation with the narcissist, try to do something positive. Eat some good food. Enjoy a nice movie. Do something you like. Prime your mind into thinking you are experiencing positive emotions.

- This might be the most important advice I can give you when conversing with a narcissist. Always be in control of your emotions. If they say something that angers you, don't show that anger on your face. Don't give them openings that they can exploit. If you feel a certain emotion bubbling to the surface, use the tactic that I mentioned earlier and excuse yourself from the conversation. Fake a task that you have to get back to, or simply let them know that you have a lot to think about. Perhaps you should continue the conversation once you both have had a chance to think things through.

When you are in the middle of a confrontation, it is easy to lose control of your emotions. Narcissists are great at poking holes in your demeanor, hoping to see you crack. They might try everything, from lies to insults to mental games. While it might seem difficult to maintain your composure, it isn't entirely impossible.

The first thing to realize is that you need to expect the worst from the narcissist. Before you even attempt to communicate with them, know that they are probably going to use plenty of tricks to dislodge your mental balance. Expect the unexpected. You are going to enter a battlefield where fair play is not the name of the game.

Once you have prepared yourself mentally, you might have a level of awareness that will help you communicate better. But when you begin communicating with the narcissist, don't focus on the harshness of their words. Instead, pay attention to the patterns they use. What kind of language do they resort to quickly? How angry do they get? What triggers them?

The last question is especially important. Sometimes, when you are receiving multiple attacks and feeling mentally exhausted, you need to turn the tables on the narcissist. This might sound like you are about to retaliate, but it isn't. What you are doing is preventing the narcissist from continuing to attack you by bringing the flow of the conversation back to its original course. You should be looking for questions that make them uncomfortable, truths that make them defensive, and suggestions that they try to deny.

You don't necessarily have to invent something fictional to respond to the narcissist. Instead, focus on the reason you are having the conversation. Prepare a list of questions that you would like to ask the narcissist. Then make a list of suggestions and a list for a few truths that you would like to discuss with them. Don't throw all the questions at the narcissist in quick succession. Make them respond to each one properly. If they try to sidetrack, then instead of responding to their new statement or question, refocus on your original train of thought.

Here's an example:

Victim: I wanted to talk to you about the way you behaved last night.

Narcissist: Really? You want to bring that up now? Is there no other time you could bring this up? Also, you act as though you hadn't done anything at all. You're not my parent. Which is apt since you can barely take care of your own life. **(This is the narcissist's way of trying to change the narrative to shift the focus to the victim.)**

Victim: I don't mind waiting for a better time to talk. When do you think you might have time? **(Notice how they are not responding to the narcissist's attack.)**

Narcissist: I don't know. What do you think I am? An oracle? Besides, I have a lot to do this week, and I don't want you stressing me out. Don't be so selfish. Maybe you might have all the free time in the world, but I don't. **(Not only are they trying to hurt the victim's**

feelings, but they are also attempting to avoid talking about the topic for as long as necessary.)

Victim: I can understand. You do have a lot of work, but if we can have a nice conversation about this, then we won't have to worry about facing it in the future when we least expect it. How about we head over to that cafe you like? **(Remember that, in this case, the victim might know the narcissist well, so they suggest a cafe because they know how public places tone down the aggressiveness of the narcissist.)**

If you look at the above conversation, then the victim is not taking the bait and retaliating. Instead, they are focused on their goal, which is to discuss the narcissist's recent behavior. Make sure that you don't place any unrealistic expectations on the conversation. For example, do not expect it to go smoothly the first time. You have to understand that things might not go the way you want them to. The narcissist might storm out, ignore you completely, or just delay the conversation. Don't be disheartened.

It's best not to expect immediate results if you are planning to have a conversation with a narcissist. Manage your expectations. You are going to embark on a long journey ahead. To prepare, pack your bags with all the essentials and train your mind. What are the essentials? Allow me to provide you with a list:

- Patience
- Mental strength
- Courage
- Confidence

- Firmness
- Understanding

Don't you worry. I am not going to just drop a list on you without letting you know how you can use each item.

Patience. Make sure that you practice patience and mindfulness. Simply put, mindfulness is the act of staying in the present and being cognizant of your environment. This is important since a wandering mind tends to travel into the past, dredging up uncomfortable and painful memories. You need to tell your mind to stop meandering and stick to the present.

Here is a simple mindfulness exercise that I recommend. You can use it anywhere, whether you are at work or home. You can even use it when you are traveling.

Make sure that you are seated with your feet firmly planted on the floor. If you are at home, you can choose to lie down. Your position does not matter as long as you are comfortable and can feel the surface beneath your hands or feet.

You can choose to close your eyes, or you can stare at a point in front of you. I assume you might not want to close your eyes on public transport. So pick a point in the distance. Just make sure you are not fixated on someone's forehead. That might be rather awkward for the other person.

Now, start by taking a few deep breaths. This is just to get you into the frame of mind for the practice. Just inhale and exhale. You don't have to worry about holding your breath.

Bring your breathing back to normal. Inhale and exhale like you always do. I would recommend focusing on your breath. A lot of us are not aware of how shallow our breathing is until we start focusing on it. If you notice your breathing comes in quick bursts, then you are not breathing properly when you are not focused on it. When I first started mindfulness exercises, I realized that my body used to hold the breath. It was automatic and a result of all the stress and negative emotions pent-up inside me.

Once you are breathing comfortably, allow yourself to focus on your abdomen. Feel the expansion and contraction as you take in a breath and release it.

At this point, you might notice thoughts flit across your consciousness. They are mostly going to be difficult memories and uncomfortable ideas. Memories of abuse, thoughts of vengeance, deep-rooted anger, and other negative thoughts burst into your mind like an unwelcome firecracker.

Don't ignore them. Simply make a mental note that they appeared, and then move on. If the thoughts are stubborn, don't force them out of your mind. Be gentle. Keep on nudging them away with kindness. After all, those thoughts are part of you. They are born out of your experiences. In many ways, they are you.

For example, just because you want to take revenge on the narcissist and hurt them badly does not make you a bad person. It just means your mind hasn't been trained to deal with painful memories. It needs your guidance. For a long time, your mind has been subject to abuse and manipulation. It is time to show it what genuine love feels like. It is time to direct some love to yourself. I have to admit if there is one thing I learned from a narcissist, it is to never stop loving oneself. Who knew they could reveal some life advice?

Continue breathing and avoiding negative thoughts. Always try to keep your attention on your breath.

When starting, perform this exercise for about five minutes. It doesn't have to be long. You can increase the duration of the exercise if you want, but it is entirely up to you. You can also use it when you require a quick mental recharge.

Mental strength. You know what they say about knowledge; it is power. When I am talking about mental strength, I am not only referring to the control you should have over your emotions but also the knowledge to give you the power to face the narcissist.

When it comes to mental health, remember to take care of yourself. Eat healthily. Sleep well (and without stress this time since I can imagine that a good night's sleep might have been difficult with the narcissist in your life). Take joy in taking care of yourself. When your mind notices how much effort you are putting in to improve yourself and the joy it brings you, it becomes hooked on that idea. In fact, your mind might start nudging you when you don't receive your daily intake of good feelings. For a long time, all your mind had seen were negative emotions, and it began to feed on that. Time to give it a different kind of mental food.

Let's not forget about knowledge. Before, you were unaware of the narcissist's personality. You might not have understood that behind all the insults and scorn, there is a person just seeking attention. Think of them as children who are loud because they want someone to look at them. In the case of children, the reaction is justified. However, in the case of a narcissist, the reaction is infantile, especially when realizing that they are capable of having more maturity. This knowledge will help you realize that you had nothing to worry about in the first place.

You can find this knowledge in many ways. This book should give you a foundation for your studies. I would also recommend paying attention to the narcissist's actions, words, and emotions. Find out how they might react or what they might say. Most importantly, pay attention to the 'why' if you can. Why did they get angry when all you suggested was doing some other activity? Why would they insult you simply because you had a different opinion? These help you piece together a bigger picture of the narcissist.

They help you realize a vital truth; narcissists are insecure inside.

Courage. Don't stop reminding yourself about the kind of person you are. More importantly, don't stop learning more about the narcissist. The more strengths you find out about yourself and the more truths you reveal about the narcissist (which are also their weaknesses), the more courage you build inside yourself.

Confidence. Keep doing the things that you enjoy. Don't let the narcissist dictate how you should be living your life. Each time you perform an act that brings joy to your life, you gain a little more confidence in being yourself.

That is powerful. A narcissist does not want you to be yourself. They want you to be *their* version of yourself.

Eventually, you will reach a point where you take joy in the things you do. You smile because you want to. You connect with people because you want them in your life. You speak in a way that matches your personality.

You become *you*, and *you* are truly special. Never forget that.

Firmness. You need to stand your ground. Do you believe that you are right? Then keep that belief planted within you.

Here is a tactic that I recommend. Before you even meet the narcissist, make sure that you know everything you had said and done. If something was your fault, admit it to yourself. Denying it only makes things difficult because when confronting the narcissist, they might pressure you about your denial. When that happens, you might not have the right responses, which, in turn, encourages the narcissist to take advantage of your hesitation. Be sure of your stance on a subject. Know what you did, and never waver because of the narcissist's words. Remember that they might attempt to throw you off.

Another method you can practice before conversing with a narcissist is to write down all the points you want to talk about. You can keep them in a note-taking app on your phone or even write them down in a notebook. It's up to you. Take the notes with you for reference. When you are talking to the narcissist, start with each point you made. If you notice that the narcissist is deviating from the topic, gently bring them back.

Here's an example.

You: I know we haven't agreed on a lot of things, but I want to know why you said those things about me to my friends.

Narcissist: What things? Listen, I just mentioned something as a lighthearted comment. It's not like I lied about it. You have been ignoring me. We meet like once a month. Don't play this down.

You: Let's talk about that. I know I might have taken some extreme steps, but I want to try to change that. Even so, we are incredible people. You have so much good in you. Do you think that we should talk about each other to our friends?

Narcissist: Please. You have nothing to talk about when it comes to me.

You: Maybe. But do you still think that people with good intentions like us should resort to something like that?

What you are doing is bringing the attention of the narcissist to the fact that they had talked about you behind your back to your friends. However, you are not blaming them directly. You are trying to let them know that you understand them and that if you had committed the same actions they did, it would still be wrong.

Do note that you are not trying to empathize with the narcissist. You don't have to, and I strongly recommend that you keep your empathy at bay. They are always waiting for an opportunity. Revealing your empathy is almost like opening the doors of your mind and rolling out the red carpet.

Understanding. In the previous example, we saw how you can be understanding without having to resort to empathy.

But are there any tricks to make sure you don't allow your empathy to slip through? There are.

One of the biggest tactics that you can use is to never—and I mean *never, ever, ever, EVER*—ask the narcissist **what you can do to help** or present similar ideas. Here is an example. If they break down, don't offer your napkin. Look for a box of tissues nearby, and if you can, pass it on to them. If you have to take extra steps to get the tissues, such as walking over to a nearby table, don't do it.

Another example could be when the narcissist talks about how they feel bad and are lonely without you. They might say that you made them a better person. Don't offer to spend more time with them. No matter how difficult it is, do not extend your hand to help them. Bite down any version of "Let me see what I can do to help." Do not allow them to surface.

Instead, you could try asking the narcissist what *they* can do to help themselves.

A few examples:

- So, what do you plan to do about it?
- How are you going to deal with this?
- What are you going to do to avoid this idea/situation/person?

Let's say that they attempt to force you into a situation where it seems as though you should help.

For example:

Narcissist: All I need is for you to continue believing in me. Let's meet up more often. I know I can change.

You: I do believe in you. That's exactly why we cannot meet more often. Why not go out there? Meet more people. Get to know them and learn to improve yourself more.

Don't be ready to offer them help. This might be particularly difficult for you if you have been close to your friend. For that, I recommend the next tip.

Spend time with more people who have a positive influence on your life. You are going to feel a sense of withdrawal as though you lost a part of yourself. You might want to hang out with your friend even more.

There might be a need to reset your relationship by giving your friend another chance.

Don't do it.

Instead, meet more people. Spend time with your family. Make new friends. The more you realize that you are capable of meeting incredible people in your life, the more your mind begins to crave the presence of those people. To be honest, that is not a bad craving at all. After all, what is so bad about being in the presence of people who appreciate you for who you are or care about you?

Eventually, you begin to gain a certain awareness. You realize you have been part of an abusive, controlling, deceitful, and false relationship. The more awareness you gain, the less empathy you develop for the narcissist. Eventually, when you are conversing with them, you don't automatically feel bad when they try to shed tears or reveal a sob story.

Even after you have gained awareness, you might sometimes feel the need to empathize. For that reason, I also recommend the next tactic.

Gain more control over your reactions and emotions. You need to understand yourself. The best way to do this is by first following the previous tactic. Surround yourself with people who are kind to you. In their presence, notice how you react to different things. What makes you happy? Why do you feel upset about certain things? What makes you sad? Analyze these behaviors because you can only do so safely with people who are not out to manipulate you.

You can also perform the above exercise in front of a narcissist. However, I would advise against it until you have gained a certain level of control over your emotions. You do not want to reveal any openings.

Additionally, take care of your body. Your physical well-being is as important as your mental well-being. You don't have to aim for a six-pack, but try to keep yourself active. Explore the outdoors. Take a walk outside. Spend time with nature.

You are more likely to be emotionally vulnerable when you have negative moods or anxiety. In fact, according to research published in the *US National Library of Medicine*, physical exercise not only helps in managing depression, anxiety, and negative moods, but it also improves cognitive function and self-esteem (Sharma et al., 2006).

You need a higher cognitive function to bypass the flood of emotions you face during stressful situations and look at your experience from an objective standpoint. Without strong cognitive capabilities, you might easily fall prey to your emotions.

Furthermore, higher self-esteem is vital if you want to place yourself in front of the needs of the narcissist. You need to be confident about yourself and value the person you are. When you can do that, the narcissist's powers of influence will diminish. Your self-esteem is the holy water to the curse of the narcissist's control.

There are a few more tips you can keep in mind when it comes to your emotions.

Remember that it is okay to feel annoyed. You don't have to pretend that you are not getting annoyed. If you do get annoyed in front of the narcissist, you have several choices. One option is to show them that you are annoyed. Let them know that you do not appreciate the way they talk to you or behave. Another option would be to first show the narcissist that you are annoyed and then walk away from the conversation. They should realize that they cannot say or do whatever they please. If they don't respect you and your time, then you don't have to stick around to respect them.

Even if they attack you, do not take their comments personally. Use the above tactic to show that you do not appreciate their verbal attacks. Then you can choose to leave the conversation.

At the same time, try to understand that they are probably saying and doing some things because they are feeling insecure. When you recognize this fact, it might help you approach a narcissist from a different perspective. If your friend truly is someone worth having in your life, then try to help them with a dose of kindness. Remember, keep your empathy to yourself. Instead of doing things for them, try to guide them. If they truly care about you as a friend, they won't be averse to changing themselves.

Keep your positivity up. Do not let the narcissist quell the good nature in you. I know this is not going to be easy, but if you have been following the tactics mentioned in this book, then you might have more control over yourself.

It is okay to take a little time to help the narcissist face their insecurities and anxieties. It is also okay to allow them to explain themselves or vent a little. But do not give them all the time for it. Remember to bring back the conversation to the points of focus.

At the same time, don't hesitate to keep your humor about you. If you think that the narcissist is being too harsh with their words or actions, then you can mention it to them with a joke. Just make sure you do not insult the narcissist because that could create an issue of its own.

Finally, see if the person needs help. By that, I don't mean you should offer your help. Don't put yourself in that position. But they might need professional help, and that is something you can suggest. If they are truly willing to change, they might consider your suggestion. In fact, professional help can help them come to terms with themselves. They can find ways to overcome their narcissistic personality.

So far, we have talked about the many ways you can approach a narcissist, but we have yet to cover an important aspect of dealing with a narcissist, how to defend yourself.

Chapter 5:

Safeguarding Yourself

I am powerful and in control of myself.

When you face a narcissist, it isn't all about how to speak to them or behave in front of them. You also need to know how to raise your shields. You need to have more power.

To Protect and to Serve

From this point onward, you are going to police your actions and behavior in front of the narcissist. And just like the Los Angeles Police Department, your motto is going to be to protect and to serve with a slightly different meaning. You are going to protect yourself. You are going to serve yourself. That is the only guideline you should know. Actually, let's not try to give any wiggle room for you to change your attitude. Let's not call it a guideline.

It is a rule. Your rule. You are going to follow it strictly, and it is a rule reserved only for the narcissist.

Because you might have to deal with the narcissist. For whatever reason—maybe the narcissist is your best friend, maybe you believe that they can change, or perhaps you cannot truly avoid them all the time—you will be interacting with the narcissist. In such scenarios, all you have to remember is the rule.

To protect *yourself* and to serve *yourself.*

Once you have added that rule to your life, it is time to move on to the actual measures to protect yourself.

Do not take anything personally. I know what you are thinking. Easier said than done, right? I wholeheartedly agree. However, once you have brought a certain peace into your life, you might also gain a certain degree of awareness. You begin to realize that a narcissist's words are hollow. Sure, they are meant to cause pain. But they have no substance. They are like blank rounds in a gun, just scare tactics. Once you realize that, you won't concern yourself with the attacks of the narcissist.

You create your own boundaries. What are your values and desires? What are the things that are important to you? Answer these questions honestly, and create boundaries accordingly. Once done, ask how much of the narcissist's behavior you are willing to tolerate. Then add in more rules for your boundaries. When finished, do not compromise on the rules of your boundaries no matter what the narcissist says or does. You are not supposed to get used to *them*. They are supposed to get used to *you.*

Create the "YOU Template." This is a practice that I created to help the victims of narcissists. Take a notebook. Yes, you need a book because a piece of paper won't cut it. I'll explain why in a bit. In this notebook, write down everything you believe about yourself. Your hopes, dreams, likes, and personality. Mention the positive components of yourself. Ask the people you trust, such as your family or other friends, what kind of person you are. Get their feedback and create a compilation of the greatest hits of you. This is your YOU Template.

You can keep adding more stuff to this book. If you ever stumble upon a piece of wisdom or a quote, add it to the book. Did you pursue a passion or a hobby? Then write down how you felt about it. Did you help somebody recently? Write down what you thought about yourself at that moment. Keep on adding as many entries into the YOU Template as possible. After all, you deserve to write so much more about yourself than what could fit on a piece of paper. Every time a narcissist makes you doubt yourself, step away from them and take out the YOU Template. Remember the wonderful human being you are.

Don't just stay silent. Advocate for your personality and behavior. Speak up when a narcissist tries to blame you for something you haven't done, lie about your traits, or change your memory about something. Correct the narcissist at that moment. If the narcissist tries to turn your response into an argument, then don't indulge them. Let them know that you are willing to talk if they can have a civilized conversation. If they fail to listen to you, just walk away. You can continue the conversation later.

Manage your interactions. If you were in the company of the narcissist often, then limit your interactions with them. On the other hand, if your interactions were sparse to begin with, then limit them even more. Take certain measures in their company. If you are with a group of friends, have a seat next to someone you are comfortable with and keep a distance from the narcissist. For a friend or colleague who works with you, find another spot in the office. If a friend had been visiting you at your home frequently, let them know that you can meet them outside beyond the walls of your place of zen. Even if you happen to see them once a month, don't be uncomfortable with that idea. If that helps you escape their grasp, then go ahead and place a limited number of interactions in your life.

Be aware of your weaknesses and vulnerabilities. One of the most important parts of a good mental defense is to understand your own openings. What makes you sad? Are you sensitive about a certain aspect of yourself (such as your weight, speech impairment, or any other debilitating factor)? Think of all these vulnerabilities. Embrace them. Acknowledge them. Most importantly, do not share them with your friend. If you have already revealed a large part of your life to your friend, then learn to accept who you are. Don't let your friend use what you have shared about yourself to mount an attack against you. The most important idea is that you should not share truths about yourself more than is necessary.

Trust yourself. Once you begin to gain an understanding of the narcissist and yourself, you develop a sense that alerts you when the narcissist attacks, lies, or tries to manipulate you. In such situations, trust your instincts. Adopt a critical lens when you are dealing with a narcissist. Learn to spot their tactics. If you believe you might have stumbled across a potential threat from the narcissist, don't try to ignore it. Listen to it and either create space between you and the narcissist or avoid coming into contact with them until you recover emotionally.

Remember to educate yourself about narcissism. You have in your hands a collection of knowledge about narcissism. Use it. Look out for red flags that scream 'narcissism.'

Block out the narcissist's personality. They might try to influence you with their charm, sadness, outgoing personality, or sense of humor. They want you to lower your defenses so that they can reach you and try influencing you again. Don't let them. If you think that something is wrong, then it more than likely is. Get out of there.

Don't let go of people in your life. The narcissist finds opportunities when you are alone. You need to let the narcissist know that you have people you can depend on. There is strength in numbers. Never hesitate to show your strength if you feel threatened.

But despite every measure you take, sometimes you might be subjected to a narcissist's abuse. Before we go any further, there is something I would like to point out.

It Is Not Okay

Abuse is abuse. If you are going through emotional or, worse, physical abuse, then please do not stay silent. You are a wonderful human being filled with hopes, dreams, and ambitions. You don't deserve to be treated like anything less than that.

Maybe you have noticed signs in your friend. They interrupt you constantly. They are critical of you or humiliate you in front of others. Their temper flares up when it comes to you, as though you had committed the biggest crime of your life against them. They might even try to scare you. Recognize these signs and speak to somebody. Reach out to your family. Seek out the help of a local support group. Do not stay silent. If you do, then you are practically recognizing the fact that abuse is okay. It isn't. It shouldn't be. Silence isn't golden. It's radioactive uranium that slowly eats away at your life. I urge you, as a friend, to never allow abuse to define your life. Don't let it change who you are and the precious beauty that lies within you. If the abuse has reached physical levels, then do not hesitate to reach out to the local abuse hotline.

As you are reading this, I would like you to evaluate the narcissistic friend in your life. Have they begun to physically abuse you in any way? Even shattering objects in your presence out of pure rage or displaying acts of violence should concern you. I urge you to place an abuse hotline on speed dial. You can even store the number of the local authorities. If you find yourself in a dangerous situation with the narcissist where your safety is threatened, reach out to one of those numbers. One tip is to call 911 and pretend that you are ordering food so that the narcissist does not become angrier by you talking to the police.

Remember to take care of yourself. You need to start loving yourself enough to realize that you deserve a spot on this planet we call Earth.

Don't Stand for Abuse

Recognize the signs of abuse. Sometimes, they might not be all that obvious, but you need to keep an eye out for them. If you notice even a small sign of abuse, do something. You can choose to walk away or confront the narcissist about it.

Abuse does not have to be physical. If your friend becomes verbally or emotionally abusive, then you need to reconsider being in their presence. Look out for the below signs of abuse as well:

- Feeling emotionally drained when you are in their presence. They are probably manipulating you to an extreme degree if you are feeling that way.
- They patronize you or humiliate you. It does not matter if they do it privately or in a public space. What you need to know is that you shouldn't stand for it.

- If they threaten you or yell at you, then they are unable to control their rage.
- When they insult you or call you names, then they are demeaning you. They want to lower your confidence so you become submissive.
- Being possessive of you or making false accusations against you. Be careful about what they tell your family or other acquaintances you know.
- Telling you what you should be feeling or how you should react at a particular moment instead of allowing you to have your own agency.
- Making it seem as though your opinions and needs do not matter.

When you notice any of the above behavior, try to distance yourself from the narcissist for a while to heal yourself. If the narcissist has a single behavior from the list above, then you can try to have a conversation with them. Help them understand themselves and what they are doing wrong. However, if they have two or more traits, then you should recommend professional help.

Always keep a close eye on your emotional and physical health. If you notice either of the two deteriorate when you are around the narcissist, then there is a high chance that they are manipulating you or trying to control you.

The Aftermath

Time is typically a measurement. We use it to count the number of hours we spend working, how long we need to wait before our next appointment, or how our tasks are progressing. We use it to meet our friends on time or let them know why they were not on time. Time also lets us know how old we are. In fact, every birthday is a reminder that you are a year older. For that reason, time can be an indication of a milestone. It shows how long you have left until your next anniversary, the fact that Christmas is just around the corner, or a sign of progress of the energy you spent doing something. On the other hand, time can be a motivator to do something. You are running late for an interview. The movie is about to start, and you still haven't gotten your popcorn.

When I have spoken to survivors of abuse, they have a vague idea of time and its influence on their lives. Typically, you might hear statements like, "I can't believe I wasted three years of my life for this person" or "I lost so much of my life because of this." To victims, time might as well cease to exist during their time with a narcissist. It feels as though one day bleeds into the next without a sign of progress, achievement, joy, or improvement.

That shouldn't be how time functions. You shouldn't be spending the rest of your life wondering why the previous years of your life were lost to you. Time shouldn't indicate the depth of the emotional trauma or abuse you went through. When that happens, you might become locked in an endless cycle of remembrance and regret.

If you have been in a narcissistic relationship and the damage has been done, don't worry. It is never too late. You can regain your life. In fact, we are going to start right now.

Firstly, **a time for recuperating.** You need to spend more time on healing and less time remembering. This is going to be a difficult balance to maintain. It is important to not speed up the healing process. Yet, at the same time, you cannot spend excessive time ruminating. While we need to address our painful memories, we also need to set aside some time for ourselves.

Here is what you need to do. Set aside a time, typically an hour each day, for ruminating. Just take this time to deal with your thoughts. Don't be ashamed of them or feel guilty. Listen to them. Heed the lessons they present. Know that no matter how painful the memories are, you never had much choice in the matter. You might find yourself chastising yourself for not taking a particular action in the past or not speaking up for yourself. It is easy to correct ourselves after a situation has passed. After all, we have all the time to correct our actions. But when you were in the middle of the situation unfolding, you had a lot to deal with.

Once the hour has passed, focus on other things that you can do, such as watching your favorite movie, working on a project, or meditating. Chances are that the painful thoughts might interrupt you, but at least their voices will be quieter.

Next, **a time for building.** Take a small part of your day to focus on your goals. Think about all the things you would like to achieve. Or perhaps you have been meaning to tackle a project you never had the chance to do before. Become the master of not just survival, but of your life's agency.

Then comes **a time for growth.** We all have a unique skill or talent that we never pay attention to. In your case, you might have lost all ideas of the skill or talent in the presence of the narcissist. Time to resurrect them.

I would like you to write down your skills and talents on a piece of paper. Once done, I would like you to list at least four or five things that you can accomplish or cultivate with each skill or talent. It does not matter if your accomplishments are small or big. Scale isn't the concern here. What matters is that you can do something about what you have with you. If you can, try to pay special attention to anything that can contribute to the betterment of others.

Take me, for example. I loved writing. When I wanted to focus more on myself, I listed writing as my skill. I then made a note of five things I would do with writing. Here's my list:

- Become a freelance writer.
- Publish a book.
- Teach others how to write (perhaps an online course).
- Write for magazines and publications.
- Create my own blog.

In a similar manner, I also tackled my talent for photography. I wasn't exactly good at it, but I enjoyed the hobby, so why not? My list included:

- Capture landscapes.
- Help photograph moments from my friends' weddings.
- Submit photographs to competitions.
- Travel the world and photograph my experiences.

You wouldn't believe it, but my friends began to notice my talent for capturing wonderful wedding photographs. I am now a freelance wedding photographer, and I launched my personal brand. It isn't anything grand, but it does feel like I have accomplished something. You may not focus on starting your own business with your skills and talents. That is okay. The point is to use them frequently. Improve them. Show that you are making progress in your life. It is a good feeling. It makes you feel powerful knowing that you made improvements all on your own.

Finally, **a time for endings.** Say goodbye to toxic relationships. You are a spectacular human being capable of making better friends. If you feel as though your relationship had taken a hefty toll on you, then take a break or break it off entirely. It is up to you. But know that ending things does not make you a coward or cruel. After all, you are walking away from abuse. What is cowardly or cruel about that?

Ignorance Is Bliss, But What If You Cannot Ignore?

Maybe you are walking down the street on your way to an appointment or you are sitting at a cafe. You are in your own comfortable space. It is a beautiful day.

Guess who turns up to ruin the moment?

Yes, indeed. It is your friendly (yeah, right) neighborhood narcissist.

What do you do in such circumstances? How can you defend yourself from what is to come? Should you just run away?

While walking away might be an option that you can consider in the worst-case scenario, you cannot keep running away from the narcissist. You cannot sacrifice everything to avoid being in the presence of someone. Your life matters. You should be able to sit at a cafe and enjoy the delicious coffee. You should be able to take a walk in the park, take the same route to work, and even hang out with other people without having to constantly scan the faces around you. Your life shouldn't be filled with fear and apprehension. So, what do you do in such a scenario?

Use the grey rock method. With this method, you become the most uninteresting person around. Essentially, you are acting like a rock. What does this look like? How do you respond when a narcissist tries to engage you? You don't. Instead, you don't react at all. In fact, you continue doing what you are doing. Don't pay attention to the narcissist in any way.

If they approach you, you can choose to acknowledge them with a short but friendly 'hello.' You don't have to initiate the conversation, nor do you have to prolong it.

Bite back your emotional responses. Keep practicing the techniques mentioned in this book to gain control over your emotions. By not revealing your emotional response, you are going to starve the narcissist's need to incite drama.

Keep your dialogue to an absolute minimum. For example, they may ask, "So what are you up to these days?" You can answer with, "Not much. Right now, I'm just trying to enjoy this cup of coffee."

Don't be hesitant to let them know that you need your space. Continuing with the example above, the narcissist might say, "Mind if I join you?" Don't hesitate to respond with, "I just want to have a quiet moment for myself right now. Some other time perhaps."

Do not talk about your personal life. No matter what they try. For example, you may be tempted to respond to the "*So what are you up to these days?*" type of question with, "Nothing much. Just focusing on my work and stuff I have to do at home." That might not be the best response because the narcissist might pursue the topic further with, "Oh, yeah? Where do you work?" Keep your personal life to yourself. The narcissist does not need to know about it.

While we are on the subject of personal life, it might be tempting to flaunt an accomplishment in their face. You might suddenly develop the urge to show the narcissist what you have done. You might feel as though the narcissist deserves their comeuppance. As tempting as that might be, do not reveal anything to the narcissist. They can be quite vindictive. Not only will they take this as a personal attack and then plan to somehow get back at you in the future, but you are revealing personal information about yourself to the narcissist. Besides, your life should not matter to them anymore. You have come so far with your achievements. Wouldn't you rather share those accomplishments with people who genuinely care about you?

While we are on the topic of not revealing too much about yourself, don't share how you are feeling either. This might be rather tricky because you can't exactly hold back from showing your emotions unless you are willing to do your best Terminator impression in front of them. Instead, I am referring to responses related to your current state. For example, the narcissist may say, "You look happy. Something good must have happened to you." Don't respond with, "Of course. Things are finally looking up, and I am feeling happy." Instead, try to throw in a casual remark, such as, "I'm just trying to enjoy this book I am reading. I'm going to get back to it now. You have a great one."

Another way to avoid dragging them into an uncomfortable conversation is to never ask them any questions. A question is an invitation. Their response may not be something you like. In fact, in some cases, the narcissist might just revel in throwing a harsh response your way. They want to dismantle your demeanor. To them, destruction is a dish best served raw, and the narcissist is going to offer the rawest version possible.

Even when you are forced to respond to them, stick to the facts. Here is an example:

Narcissist: So, are you heading somewhere?

Your response (FACT): I am just taking a walk.

Narcissist: Oh, that's fantastic. I actually am walking myself. Should we head over to where you are going together?

Your response (FACT): No, I want to have this moment by myself. I'll take this walk alone.

Narcissist: It will be fun. Come on.

Your response (FACT): I mean it. I do want to be left alone.

Remember, you don't have to offer facts if you think they are too personal. If the narcissist asks what you are doing with your life, you don't have to provide an answer. That part of your life is yours alone. You can share it with people you genuinely trust. If the narcissist insists on knowing about your life, then you can hit them back with another fact, such as, "I don't want to talk about it. Please don't ask." It is the truth, and sometimes, you just need to hand it to them directly.

Also, make sure that you don't make references to the past. Do not reminisce or remember events that have already happened. Let the past stay exactly where it should be, in your memories. Talk about the present. I would even go so far as to recommend that you not talk about the future either. Whatever you have planned, you can keep it to yourself. But what if the narcissist talks about the past? Well, here is a situation and how you can handle it.

Narcissist: It's great to see you at this cafe. Remember the times we used to always come for the caramel latte during lunch hours? Time flies.

You (Option 1): Say nothing and simply offer a smile. No need to reminisce along with them. Let them delve into their past. Your life is in the present.

You (Option 2) say: Yes. But I have to get back to this coffee. Catch you sometime.

You could even combine the above two approaches. Firstly, you could remain silent for a short while. Then you could remark on how you should get back to what you were doing.

Don't hesitate to be firm. Your time is valuable. It is not a currency that can be doled out freely. If your time was part of the currency market, you need to make sure it is a truly good exchange rate. Your valuable time for someone else's valuable time. Don't cheapen yourself. You are much better than that.

Questions, Questions, Questions

Sometimes, you can avoid interacting completely or may decide to end the relationship with a narcissist. Other times, you might want to ask yourself whether you would like to continue with the relationship or the interaction you were having. Here are a few questions that can help you decide. There are two sections to this questionnaire. The first section focuses on questions that ask you to explain how you think or feel in the presence of the narcissist. In the second section, you are going to evaluate the absence of the narcissist.

Presence

- What does it cost me to be in the presence of the narcissist or tolerate their behavior?
- How much am I giving and how much am I receiving in return?
- How exhausted do I feel when I am in the presence of the narcissist?
- What kind of emotions do I experience?
- What memories flood my mind?
- What kind of thoughts come to me? Do I feel like I want to slap the narcissist right across the face? Do I think of running away?
- What will I gain if I continue this relationship with the narcissist?

Absence

- What might it cost me should I ever decide to not be in the presence of the narcissist?
- What will I gain if I leave the narcissist or stop interacting with them?
- Will I be able to accomplish the things that I want in their absence?
- How am I going to feel now that the narcissist is not in my life anymore?
- How dependent was I on the narcissist when I was in their presence?
- What do I feel now without the narcissist being around me?
- Is it important for me to be in the presence of the narcissist right now?

If you come across a situation where a narcissist contacts you to spend time with them, then you can use the absence questionnaire. It might help you decide whether you would truly like to meet the narcissist or not.

Remember, even if you go for months without meeting them, do not feel guilty about it. The time you need for healing is different from the time I require. If you start experiencing anxiety at the thought of meeting them, then you are more than likely not ready to be in their presence. During this period, they might start to contact you or try to make you feel guilty about your actions. Don't fall for their words or ideas. In fact, the very fact that they are trying to implant guilt, sadness, anger, frustration, or any other negative emotion in you shows their intentions. You don't have to return to that.

Of the Body and the Mind

Sometimes, the narcissist might be going through serious mental health issues. If you have noticed long periods of depression or if your friend displays extreme levels of narcissism, then you should recommend professional help. Remember, don't try to *be* the professional help. That is not your job. Understanding over empathy.

At the same time, I would also like you to focus on your mental health. How are you feeling? Are you prone to depression? Do you need medication just to sleep well? Evaluate your mental health and see if you might need professional help as well.

I know what some of you might think—you don't need help.

Getting professional help does not make you look weak, crazy, or odd. It simply means that you want to get better. You want the dark cloud hanging over your mind to disappear and bring in the rays of sunshine. It isn't an easy choice to make when you decide to seek out a therapist.

When I was challenging my abusive relationship, I was against the idea of a professional looking at me. Thoughts of wearing a straightjacket crossed my mind, and I felt as though I was somehow psychotic. That I was dangerous. Over time, I realized something truly important.

I just wanted to get better. I wanted to regain control of my life.

There is nothing wrong with admitting that you need help. There is this beauty inside you that is just waiting to burst out. Kindness, creativity, wit, ambition, determination, courage, curiosity, and ideas are just buried six feet under in your mental ground. All of your qualities simply want to come alive. They want a resurrection. Part of bringing out the best in you involves taking care of yourself.

Remember, you cannot solve a problem that does not exist. You need to admit that you need help, and that is okay.

Let someone who understands the mind help you gain control over yours.

Imagine being stranded in the middle of the highway because your car broke down. A few people pass you by and offer help, but out of apprehension, frustration, or pride, you reject all the help you receive. You then spend an hour working on the car, dismantling things and putting them back together. Yet for all your work and examinations, nothing happens. You are no better than when you started working on the engine.

If only you had asked for help.

Your mind is the car. It has broken down, not of your own accord. The narcissist's words and actions have taken their toll.

All you have to do is accept the help.

When your mental car is ready to move again, you can then focus on something grand and important.

The journey ahead.

Chapter 6:

Helping Your Friend

I am a person who is capable of having good friends.

A good friend is one who adds meaning to your life. They are the ray of hope when things look like they are about to enter the worst stage of Armageddon. They are the Batman to your mental city of Gotham. You can trust them to be there by your side, make you smile, and just spend a good time with you.

But above everything, do you know one of the best parts of a good friend? It is the fact that they accept you for who you are. They know your faults. They have gotten used to your ups and downs. When you were happy, they were there to cheer you on. At your lowest point, they were there to pick you up. They are the peanut butter if you are the jam. Or you both could be Iron Man and Captain America. Or Bonnie and Clyde. You can take your pick among the most popular duos out there.

The point is that you have accepted your friend's faults as well. They are rough around the edges, but they are someone you cherish and love. You appreciate them for who they are.

If that is indeed the case, then trying to decide whether you would like to walk away from your friend or stay and help them might be challenging. You are unsure whether you should be more understanding or raise your defenses. Should you scorn them or offer to guide them? It's an emotional conundrum because you are choosing between the need to free yourself from a harmful or abusive narcissistic influence and abandoning your friend when they might need your help.

That is why, before we even think about helping your friend, we should figure out which of the two choices you should be making. Should you gain your freedom or stick around to help?

Here's a bigger question. How can you know if your friend is suffering or the cause of your suffering?

There is a way to find that out.

Going Through the Motions

You need to first give yourself some space. Take a moment to step away from your friend for a while. Give yourself a mental detox. You can be forthcoming with your friend and let them know that you need some time to think things over. If they truly care, then they will give you that space.

When you have the moment to yourself, then you can go through the tactics mentioned in Chapter 4. Make sure that you are giving yourself enough attention. Take care of yourself.

Once you have healed sufficiently, then you can sit down to evaluate your friend's words and actions.

Here is a list of questions that you can answer about the narcissist. Do remember that this questionnaire is only to gain a better understanding of your friend. You cannot use it as a professional diagnosis. In the end, what you are trying to do is figure out a way to either help your friend or stop staying in touch with them.

- Have they constantly criticized you to nitpick your ideas, decisions, words, and actions? Whenever they carried out such actions, did it mostly feel as though they were trying to demean you?

- Do they enjoy raining on your parade? Have you felt that you are never free to express your accomplishments because you are worried about your friend's reaction?

- Are they usually challenging your moral codes, life experiences, belief systems, and core values, even when it is not needed? Do they play the devil's advocate when you never asked them to?

- Have you noticed them trying to compete with you on nearly everything? For example, you might have a good collection of classic rock tunes, and all of a sudden, your friend seems to have them too. Perhaps you might know some cool facts, and you notice that your friend has a renewed interest in them, going so far as to show off in front of your family or other friends as a show of superiority.

- Does it always seem as though their problems are worse than yours? You could be talking about something horrible that happened to you, and they have a story that is somehow worse. This is especially noticeable when you are in large groups since that would mean that the narcissist receives more attention.

- Has your friend tried to make you feel guilty when you could not do something they wanted? Notice if this happens during those circumstances when you absolutely could not help them. For example, you might be heading home from work thoroughly exhausted. Your friend asks for a drink. In your tiredness, you forget the drink. Yet instead of understanding, they make a big deal out of it as though you have somehow deprived them of something precious.

- Does your friend mistreat you and then somehow turn things around to blame you for something or make you feel guilty?

- Do they rarely apologize for their faults or take responsibility for their actions?

- Is your friend usually sarcastic toward you? You might notice this more often when you are the one attracting more attention or when it seems you are better than your friend at something.

- Has your friend tried to micromanage your affairs? Do they try to tell you what you should do, how to do it, what you should say, or how you should behave?
- Have they displayed frustration, anger, or even rage when you criticize them or offer feedback?

I would like you to understand that having just one or two of the above traits should not be of too much concern. For example, maybe your friend does not like being criticized, but they have always encouraged you to do what you want. They have supported your progress and have been happy about your accomplishments. If that is the case, then perhaps your friend has low self-esteem issues.

However, if they possess at least five of the above traits, then your friend might be showing extreme narcissistic behavior to you. In such scenarios, you can choose how you would like to approach the situation. Even then, you may not have to discontinue your relationship with your friend.

You could let your friend know that you intend to remain their friend, but they cannot control you. They cannot tell you how often you should spend time with them. You are free to meet them when you like, and you are free to do the things that you enjoy. If your friend truly cares about you, they will understand. They will be supportive of your decision.

On the other hand, if you have chosen to help your friend, there are ways you can do it.

A Friend Indeed

It isn't easy being friends with a narcissist, but it is not impossible. Your first thought should be to ask yourself why you would like to remain friends with them. Make a list of those factors.

Perhaps your list might look something like this:

- I enjoy their company.
- They have been there when I needed them the most.
- Their confidence is inspiring.

Add as many factors as possible to your list. At this point, you don't have to try and edit any point or omit them. Add them as they come to your mind.

When you are done, check how long your list is. If you feel that it is long, then try to remove some factors based on a few criteria:

- If they are providing you something, can you not find it by yourself?
- Do you need to depend on your friend for that?
- Are they doing that for you or because it serves them?
- Is that factor truly important to decide whether you would like to maintain or leave the relationship?
- Is your friend the only one capable of offering you that?

I can understand that some questions might seem harsh. However, when you begin to eliminate factors, you get an idea of why you truly want to be with your friend. Then I would like you to take the time to think for yourself. Are the factors enough for you to deal with their narcissism? Ask yourself if the benefits of maintaining your friendship outweigh the downsides of your friend's narcissism.

If you are still reading this, then perhaps you have chosen to hold on to that friendship. It is time to understand something about change.

Change May Not Be Inevitable

Perhaps the most challenging journey for a narcissist is the one they take toward change. Remember what I mentioned about problems? You can only solve them if you have chosen to admit they exist. It is the same for the narcissist. They can change. Of that, there is no doubt. However, do they *want* to change? They have to first admit that they have been hurting others, manipulating them, deceiving them, or taking advantage of them. That is a truth that many cannot easily swallow.

Once they have accepted the truth, they then have to decide if they would like to seek help. If you notice your friend examining their behaviors, reflecting on their past actions, or asking you about what they have done wrong, then they have taken a step in the right direction. They indeed want to change. They want to be a better friend.

But be warned. You should not be forcing them to come to that conclusion. You should not threaten them or try to target them personally because you feel it is good for them. Do not push them to make a decision. Inform them of what your intentions are, and let them make the decision on their own.

The question then arises, how can you inform them of your intentions? How can you guide them without coercing them?

Firstly, you need to be honest. You need to have a genuine conversation with them about their personality. Help bring their narcissism to light. Sometimes, people suffering from narcissism may not be aware that they have such tendencies. I am not talking about deep physical and psychological abuse. Please, do not justify abuse. Plan your exit strategy and then take it. Do not look back, no matter what happens. You deserve better. However, I am referring to narcissistic traits such as looking down on you, offending you repeatedly with sarcasm, or trying to dominate the conversation. Those are some of the traits that the narcissist might find normal. It is up to you to let them know that they have, in fact, been hurting you in many ways.

If you feel as though you don't know how to have that conversation with them or have tried and failed to see any results, then try a professional intervention. Inform the narcissist about going to a professional therapist. Let them know that you wish to have a genuine conversation with them, but it would be wise to have a professional's opinion. Most importantly, let them know that you are only offering them the idea of professional help because you don't want to say something that might hurt them.

More importantly, the idea of professional help—or even a personal one, for that matter—isn't to ostracize your friend. You are not trying to make light of their challenges. Instead, you are hoping to have a genuine conversation with them. Your aim is to find ways to help them understand themselves.

However, this whole process might just be a case of "easier said than done." If the narcissist stubbornly refuses to go in for professional help or rejects the idea that they have narcissism, then try to exercise the below approaches. I have provided two direct approaches and two indirect ones. You can pick one—or you can choose multiple approaches—depending on your situation.

Direct - The Separation Method

In this method, you need to catch the narcissist in the act. This method depends on actually experiencing narcissistic behavior. It might not fit a situation where you have decided to intervene and have a conversation since the narcissist can be guarded in such situations. However, you can apply this method when you are spending time with your friend.

The moment you notice a narcissistic behavior, call it out. If you are in a public space, then let the narcissist know that you would like to have a private word with them. Take them somewhere private.

You separate the behavior from the person. Don't say anything along the lines of "Did you know you were a narcissist back there?"

Instead, you could use this option or something similar: "Did you know you *acted* like a narcissist?"

What you are doing is not accusing the person directly. The first statement makes it sound like the person cannot change. You are essentially letting the narcissist know that it is them you would like to talk about. You have unintentionally made the situation personal.

The second statement, on the other hand, lets them know that you did not like their actions. The best part about actions is that they can change. You can talk about them freely. The action can be detached from the person since they are capable of taking different actions.

Do note that the narcissist might try to deny any wrongdoing. They might insist that they were in the right or that you misunderstood what they actually meant to say or do. I recommend that you don't accept their word for it. Instead, have a deeper discussion.

Ask them why they think their actions weren't narcissistic. Question them on why they think you have misunderstood.

Direct - The Single Question

Remember the single question that psychologists asked narcissists? You can use that to start a conversation with your friend. Simply ask them directly.

"Do you think that you are a narcissist?" or "Are you a narcissist?"

Allow them to answer. Based on their response, you can then ask them further questions.

Indirect - The Clarification Technique

In this method, you can draw the attention of the narcissist to their behavior by offering them clarifying questions, typically about an action or their behavior. For example, if you notice that the narcissist is humiliating you in front of your friends, then take them aside and ask them questions about their behavior.

You could ask:

- Do you think that it was okay to do that?
- Why did you feel you had to make fun of me in front of my friends?
- Does it seem fair to you that you had to bring me down?
- What would you do if I made fun of you the same way you made fun of me?
- Is this going to happen every time we are with my friends?

By presenting probing questions, you are asking the narcissist to reflect upon themselves. You can use this method during your intervention as well. Let us say that the narcissist had tried to control your behavior recently. They had been very particular about your actions, taking them apart and trying to enforce *their* ideas about how *you* should behave. During your intervention, ask questions about that.

You could ask:

- Why do you feel compelled to control my life? Do you think you have a better idea of how I am supposed to live?
- The other day, you tried to push your views about how I should live onto me. It was unsettling. Do you think that was okay on your part?
- Why did you think that your idea of how to live my life was better than my own?
- I trust you. But what you did yesterday showed me that you don't value that trust. Why did you feel you had to do it?

Remember, do not directly attack them. Always add in words such as 'think' and 'feel' to make sure that you are referring to their actions rather than them. There is a big difference between saying "Why did you do it?" and "Why did you feel that you had to do it?"

Indirect - The Humor Comeback

Many years ago, I visited my friend's place for a get-together. It was a casual event, and the evening went fairly smoothly. Fairly. There was a narcissist in the group. She wasn't behaving badly. However, my friend had ordered pizzas for all of us. The narcissist immediately pounced on the food, attempting to fill up her plate with as many slices as possible. My friend made an announcement at that moment, "Make sure everyone gets a slice." The narcissist responded with sarcasm, her plate already holding four slices, "I think we'll be good." My friend—she had copious amounts of good-natured wit—responded with, "I'm sure you are. Isn't that what's important?"

Hearing this, the narcissist casually tried to put back the slices as though she hadn't taken any in the first place. She had become aware of her actions.

Whether you are talking to the narcissist during an intervention or when they have done something to offend you, use humor to your advantage.

For example, if you had pointed out a fault to a narcissist, and they responded with, "But I didn't do anything like that."

You could respond with, "Well, the last time I checked, you didn't have a twin."

You are just accepting what the narcissist says. At the same time, you are not being rude to them. You want to let them know that you are aware of what they did. However, you are giving them the chance to come clean.

The Good, the Bad, And the Worse

Perhaps you have decided to help your friend with their NPD.

You are aware of how extreme their narcissism is. Yet you would still like to offer them a helping hand despite everything you know about them. Let me tell you I won't try to stop you. I would, however, ask you to take care of yourself first, no matter the circumstances. I know that life presents us with difficult choices. You have decided to take a course of action to help your friend. That is noble indeed.

But it is prudent to know how you can go about doing that.

Firstly, do not try to solve their problem on your own. It won't do either of you any good. You need to find a therapist or a mental health expert. Look for professionals who specialize in NPD.

I know you might think that perhaps all your friend needs is a dose of good old-fashion love. But if you truly want to help your friend, then you need to let a professional bring their brevity, precision, and expertise to the table.

At the same time, you need to prepare yourself for the worst, which is that you have to stay with your friend for the long haul. Therapy does not fix things within a week, month, or even a few months. You have to stop placing a determinate time frame on recovery. Your friend will recover when they recover. There are no shortcuts.

It is during the therapy that your good old-fashion love comes in. Your friend might try to convince you that they are well. They might ask to quit professional treatment. But until you hear from the professional themselves, do not conclude the process. Encourage your friend. Show them how much progress they have made. Offer them validation.

Know that it isn't just within the walls of the professional's place of work that therapy takes place. Recovery is a constant progress. This means that you cannot let their behavior go unnoticed. If they start making excessive self-serving remarks, point it out to them. Let them know the focus of their treatment.

Finally, make sure that you are protecting yourself as well. The narcissist is going to be tempted to poke fun at you, humiliate you, or even try to undermine you. Whatever their tactics may be, do not react emotionally. Use the previous tip to point out their behavior. Have a conversation with them about how they shouldn't revert to past behaviors if they ever hope to succeed with the treatment.

You are going to go through some good moments of triumph, you might experience bad moments of failure, and you might be part of some of the worst emotional situations for the narcissist (since they are being made to change their personality considerably). Through all that, it is your support that will guide them. They are relying on you, even though they might not openly admit it. Deep down, they might know how hard you are trying. Even though their narcissistic tendencies surface, it makes them feel guilty little by little.

We have seen what you are supposed to do to help the narcissist improve themselves. What about the narcissist? Is there something that they should be doing? Are there tactics that you can tell them to follow to ensure they are making progress?

Counterattack

It's time to go on the offensive. There are steps the narcissist can take that are typically mentioned by the therapist, but it is worth noting them here as well. These steps help your friend counter their narcissism. They help them adopt new habits and ideas that are based on understanding, empathy, and compassion.

Firstly, they need to acknowledge your boundaries. You can have a discussion about these boundaries. For example, you tell the narcissist about the below rules:

- No interrupting you when you are at work.
- You would like to have some time to yourself.
- You are not obligated to meet them every time they call you.

You might have your own set of rules, but you need to list them out somewhere and give that list to the narcissist. You are going to keep a copy of that list as well.

You are then going to check the progress of your boundaries. In other words, how often does the narcissist adhere to them?

For example, maybe you have a boundary like, "You should allow me to speak in front of my friends without interrupting." You are then going to write down the number of times the narcissist has disrespected your boundaries. Every time they try to talk over you in front of your friends or attempt to shift the spotlight to themselves, you are going to make a note of that moment. At the end of the month, you are going to show them the number of times they have broken the rules of your boundaries. This will allow you to have a healthy discussion with them on how they can improve.

The next month, you are going to repeat the process. At the end of the month, if you notice an improvement, then you know that the narcissist is trying. If, however, you realize that they haven't shown progress, then that will help you have a different kind of conversation with the narcissist. You can also bring it up with the therapist.

As you begin to keep a record of their progress, help them understand that there is a good side to themselves. Teach them to listen to your and the professional's voice. Narcissists are entranced by their inner voice. We have seen what that voice is capable of. You need to encourage them to detach themselves from their seductive but dangerous inner monologue.

Let them know that if they hear the voice in their head asking them to do something, feel in a particular manner, or use a certain phrase, then they can question it. They need to ask themselves if the suggestions they received need to be followed. The more they learn to question these voices, the faster they can gain control over their minds.

You can also let them know that the inner commentator is merely a result of their memories and emotions. They are not the narcissist's actual point of view.

One of the most effective ways to quiet the inner voice is through compassion. They can counter the statements made in their head with questions that reflect kindness. For example, if the inner voice is telling them to lie to their friend, the narcissist can respond with, "Why would I do that? They are my friend. I don't want to break their trust, and I know that honesty is going to build the trust between us."

Compassion can also be in the form of acceptance. The narcissist needs to accept that they are the same as everyone else. They are part of the human race, where each person may be unique, but they are still human. This makes us all view each other with a degree of humility and understanding. We know to not judge the people around us. We know that, just like us, they have their own struggles. They have navigated their own obstacles. Some have failed. Others have succeeded. But in the end, we all move forward. Our common humanity is what binds us in the end.

This idea of humanity can also help the narcissist practice some common habits that will help them. Here is a list:

- Make eye contact as much as possible when talking to people.
- Use the names of people when addressing them.

- Never share opinions about others behind their back. If you have something to talk about, have a straightforward conversation with the person themselves.
- Avoid lying to someone as much as possible.
- Listen more than you talk. More importantly, do not listen to respond. Listen because you want to hear what the other person is saying. Grasp the meaning of their words.
- Do not fake curiosity. Show genuine interest in people.
- Compliment others when necessary. Do not take away the spotlight when they are talking about themselves.
- If someone is in pain or discomfort, offer sympathy or help.
- Take a moment to celebrate someone's milestones. If it is someone's birthday, call them to wish them a happy birthday.
- If someone says something in anger, do not respond in kind. Step away and take a moment to calm down.
- Never hold prejudices for long. Do not plot against people.
- When making promises, stay true to your word. Be accountable. Take responsibility.
- Make small changes in relationships and at work. For example, put in a genuine effort to accomplish a task at work rather than making someone else do it.

It might be difficult for a narcissist to follow all the guidelines in the list above. But it is as they say, perfection comes from constant practice. It is through practice that they can gain a lot, including:

- A solid reputation among friends as a reliable person.
- A reputation as someone who respects others.
- A good moral compass.
- Someone who is known as being full of integrity.

The more the narcissist overrides their previous persona with new guidelines, the more they become used to their new life. The genuine respect from their friends will fill them with joy unlike what they experienced by using their narcissistic tendencies. They will realize that they no longer have to depend on manufactured attention. The look on their friends' faces and the reactions they receive because of just being a genuine person will enthrall them.

Apart from slowly practicing positive qualities, the narcissist can also learn to develop an opposing voice to their inner one. You can call this the 'observer.'

Whenever the narcissist feels compelled to say or do something that is fueled by their narcissistic tendencies, then ask them to use the following questions:

- How would someone feel about the words I am about to say or the actions I am about to take?
- Am I going to use the person because of what I am going to do?

- Are my actions going to humiliate, embarrass, sadden, anger, or hurt the person?
- Am I going to focus on myself right now, making it seem as though I am the superior one or better than that other person?

Each narcissist might have a unique set of questions based on their traits and personality. You can help your friend make a list of questions that they can use whenever they feel as though their inner voice is nudging them toward poor behavior. They can then run through those questions in their mind whenever they are in doubt.

You should also let the narcissist know that during their self-evaluation, they do not have to be critical about themselves. Encourage them to be self-forgiving, no matter how many times they have to do it. Their journey is a challenging one. They will need all the motivation they can get from you and from themselves.

As they are running through the questions, let them know that they don't have to lambast themselves for thinking in a particular manner. It isn't their inner thoughts that are important; it is their willingness to deal with their narcissistic nature that they should celebrate.

Besides taking care of yourself and helping the narcissist understand their feelings, you should also be aware of the steps in narcissism treatment. These steps will help you understand your friend and keep realistic expectations of their treatment.

Step 1: Appeasement

This is going to be the first step in most cases. Your friend won't believe in the treatment. They might go to the therapist for a quick fix for certain unpleasant emotions or just to make you happy. As soon as they feel good or notice that you are satisfied, then they are likely to quit the treatment. In some cases, your friend might walk away from the professional's office as well. Be ready to keep their focus on track.

Step 2: Self-Serving Benefits

This might be the first step in some scenarios. The narcissist might come to accept the treatment, believing in its benefits. However, they are still thinking about themselves at this point. They don't care about their actions toward others. They want the treatment to avoid pain.

Step 3: Defenses

During this step, the narcissist begins to understand the various defense mechanisms that they have set up in their lives. These mechanisms are explored without passing any judgment on the narcissist.

Step 4: New Defenses

The therapist might try to set up new defenses to override the previous ones. These defenses are there to help the narcissist understand that they can live their lives by taking into consideration the emotions of others.

Step 5: New Habits

It doesn't stop at just the defenses. The therapist will teach the narcissist to form new habits that will serve to override old behavioral patterns. For example, if they are the type to constantly interrupt someone, then they will be told to count backward from a certain point. The idea is to prevent them from reacting instinctively. By giving themselves more time to reflect on their actions, they receive more time to bring their impulses under control.

But do note that the trick is repetition. The habit might not form until it has been performed plenty of times. Repeat a few hundred times, and then the habit will stick. Eventually, the narcissist won't be able to even think of reverting to their old habit.

Step 6: Ponder Actions

Once new habits have settled in, the narcissist will be tasked with understanding the feelings of others. This doesn't necessarily mean that they are going to develop empathy. It only means that they are getting acclimated to understand the impact of their actions on others. In many scenarios, steps five and six might be merged. This is to ensure that the narcissist is forming new habits and that they can understand just why they are doing so.

Step 7: Pain

When they have sufficiently trained themselves to reflect on their actions, the narcissist will be more self-aware. At this point, the therapist might attempt to focus on past trauma and pain if they exist. The idea is to get to the root of the problem rather than simply trimming away at the weeds of behavior that might resurface in the future.

Step 8: Inner Voice Version 2.0

At this stage, the therapist might attempt to talk to the narcissist about their inner voice. What is it telling them to do? Has it become a much kinder voice? Does it show compassion? Can the narcissist rely on it to make their lives better?

Step 9: Empathy

This is one of the biggest steps for a narcissist. Up until this point, they have never put themselves in someone else's shoes. Understandably, they might be quite hesitant about going through this step, but there are a few guidelines that can help them:

- They have to realize that their friends are not a threat to them. In this case, they have to realize that you mean no harm to them.
- They should attempt to find similarities between themselves and the other person. They should find out how the other person reminds them of themselves.
- Others have experienced pain and loss as well. Many times, narcissists will be asked to talk to someone who has gone through some of the life experiences they have. For example, if they have deep depression, then they might be asked

to join anonymous groups for depression. They will be tasked with simply listening to the stories of others and reflecting on how some of those stories bear similarities to their lives.

After a number of attempts, the narcissist will finally be able to develop empathy in real life.

Step 10: No-Narcissistic Authenticity

Finally, the narcissist will be tasked with developing a genuine personality. This might be a rather frightening proposition for them. After all, they have been used to one kind of personality. Their character traits are linked with narcissism. If that ceases to exist, then what is genuine? Were they ever themselves? It is a frightening thought. When a person realizes that their identity was nothing but toxic and not a reflection of their true selves, then they begin to wonder if they have ever had a moment in their lives when they were themselves. They feel like a program that was given instructions.

This step requires patience. The narcissist will attempt to put everything they learned into practice. Over time, they will discover quirks and habits that remove their previous version.

I would also like to remind you that many therapists may not follow the steps in order. They might skip a step altogether or rearrange the order. In some cases, they might introduce a step of their own. Do not interrupt their work. Allow them to help the narcissist. It isn't too far-fetched to say that narcissism is like a fingerprint; no two personalities are exact. The therapist has to learn to tailor their methods to the patient they are dealing with.

Another important point that I would like to mention is that if your friend has NPD, then there isn't a cure for it (WebMD, 2020). This does not mean that it is all gloom and doom. There are steps that people with NPD can take to keep their negative impulses under control. Long-term treatment can keep those impulses subdued. Even today, researchers and psychologists are devising various ways to treat NPD. Until they find a definitive cure, it is important to understand that recovering from NPD is a lifelong progress.

For that reason, I urge you to practice protection methods. Keep yourself safe. Know your boundaries. Don't be afraid to speak up. If you would like to do things by yourself, go ahead. Take a holiday to an exotic location all by yourself if you must. You need to live your life on your terms too. That is the best way to help your friend as well. If your friend with NPD realizes that you are your own person, they won't exercise their narcissistic tendencies, which, in turn, helps them focus on their recovery.

You should also be aware of various therapies that are used for treating narcissism. Knowing that such therapies exist means that you won't have to rely on just one avenue of treatment. A holistic approach might just be the trick to helping your friend.

A popular therapy that is frequently recommended for people with a high degree of narcissism is cognitive behavioral therapy (CBT). The narcissists are trained to examine their distorted beliefs so that they can change their outlook. This therapy is specifically made to help narcissists lead normal and happy lives.

Another method is psychoanalytic psychotherapy, which focuses on talk-based sessions that aim to bring repressed emotions and thoughts to the surface. The main aim is to reveal the underlying problems that fuel narcissism and then address those issues directly. In this method, the therapist and patient relationship is crucial. As a friend, you might have minimal participation in the process, which is okay. You are helping your friend. Allow them to completely focus on their therapy.

Psychotherapies can exist in various forms. Among them, mentalization therapy is a popular method, and it can even be applied to our personal lives. The method focuses on thinking about your thoughts. In other words, you take the time to examine the voice in your head and understand why it chooses to present you with certain ideas, responses, memories, and words. You are then able to make better sense of your beliefs, thoughts, emotions, and wishes.

You can also choose dialectical behavioral therapy (DBT), which is a cognitive therapy that encourages the narcissist to live in the moment, examine their surroundings, be aware of their words and actions, and manage their emotions. Initially, DBT was created to serve as an effective treatment for borderline personality disorder (BPD), but over time, psychologists realized that it could be applied to other disorders and psychological conditions as well. There are various forms of DBT. One method is called Gestalt therapy, where the professional focuses on the present. Their approach is to guide the narcissist to examine their emotions and thoughts based on what is happening around them rather than what might have happened in the past.

Group therapy allows your friend to examine themselves based on the experiences of others. They can understand how others perceive them and realize that they are not alone. Sometimes, narcissists feel as though their struggle is unique. They might feel like the odd one out. Group therapy helps instill the idea that others are going through the same challenges as them.

Help Them Help Themselves

But no matter how many tactics, therapies, and ideas I offer you, they will show no progress if the narcissist is not willing to put in the effort. If your friend has decided that no matter what you say, they are okay and don't need help, then I would like you to stop pushing them. Instead, take a break and ask yourself if you would truly like to put in the effort.

I am not asking you to give up. Rather, I want you to be aware of your time and effort. If you are spending more time convincing your friend to seek help instead of leading your own life, then you are drawing yourself back into the circle of the narcissist's influence. In fact, your friend might just be addicted to the attention that you give them. They might even slingshot between decisions, going from consideration to rejection and back again. Their motive isn't to change. Instead, they have found a new way to exercise their impulses.

Furthermore, the biggest component is you. We have to understand that your healing is as important as the narcissist's. If your friend refuses to make a decision about therapy or help, then do not give them your time. Focus on yourself. Your friend might reach out to you, perhaps to let you know that they have reconsidered. Ask them to make an appointment with a professional because that is the only way you are going to believe them.

This idea of self-focus should also apply during the treatment phase. Do not spend every waking moment trying to make sure that the narcissist is okay. You are not the caretaker of their lives. In fact, nearly every therapy focuses on the narcissist's efforts. They have to go through the steps themselves. Sure, you can offer moral support, but make sure that support does not interfere with your work, life, relationships, and happiness. You deserve to live a life of your own. It is as precious as the narcissist's need to change.

You matter. But you should matter first. The life you lead, the hopes you hold, the dreams you create, and the memories you form all come together to form the character called you. Do not let go of them.

Conclusion

I am me.

You are powerful. Perhaps you may not realize that when under the narcissist's influence. But you have the power to decide how you feel and react. You may be serving the narcissist for a number of years, or you may be in their presence for a few months. It does not matter. What is important to note is that they have been, either obviously or subtly, using you for their own demands.

I would like you to know that you are not responsible for their behavior. Nor have you caused them to become who they are, if they ever try to pin their issues on you. In this relationship, you are the victim of their tendencies. Even if you decide to help them, detach yourself from their needs and wants; those are areas that the narcissist should explore themselves.

I am mentioning all of this because you need to love yourself. The journey ahead toward recovery can be arduous and challenging. But I know that you will prevail. I believe in you.

My journey was not an easy one. Often, I would find myself justifying my husband's behavior. I would say things like, "But deep down, he is a good man" or "I know his real nature, and there is kindness within him." However, I realized that by defending my husband, I wasn't helping him bring to the surface those inner qualities that I believed in. Instead, I was giving him the encouragement to stick to his surface-level narcissistic impulses. After all, I was there to defend him. He knew that. He counted on it.

After all of the lessons I have learned, I can tell you to trust yourself. Sure, you might stumble along the way to progress. But failure on the road to progress is worth it. Don't ever give up on yourself.

You are deserving of the many things that you had hoped and wished for. You are not the source of a narcissist's supply of attention. You are not theirs to own.

You are you.

I hope that this book has helped you gain a level of awareness surrounding your friend's behavior. I hope that you can use this book to turn your life around. If you have made progress or found changes in your life, then leave a review on Amazon and help others find this book.

From one survivor of a narcissistic relationship to another, I hope you gain the freedom that you seek.

References

American Psychiatric Association. (2013). Desk reference to the diagnostic criteria from DSM-5. American Psychiatric Publishing.

BBC. (2012, February 21). Dolphins deserve same rights as humans, say scientists. BBC News. https://www.bbc.com/news/world-17116882#:~:text=Dolphins%20should%20be%20treated%20as

Casale, S., Fioravanti, G., & Rugai, L. (2016). Grandiose and Vulnerable Narcissists: Who Is at Higher Risk for Social Networking Addiction? Cyberpsychology, Behavior, and Social Networking, 19(8), 510–515. https://doi.org/10.1089/cyber.2016.0189

Firestone, L. (2006). Suicide and the Inner Voice. Cognition and Suicide: Theory, Research, and Therapy., 119–147. https://doi.org/10.1037/11377-006

Foster, J. D., Shiverdecker, L. K., & Turner, I. N. (2016). What Does the Narcissistic Personality Inventory Measure Across the Total Score Continuum? Current Psychology, 35(2), 207–219. https://doi.org/10.1007/s12144-016-9407-5

Golbeck Ph.D., J. (2014, September 18). Internet Trolls Are Narcissists, Psychopaths, and Sadists. Psychology Today. https://www.psychologytoday.com/us/blog/your-online-secrets/201409/internet-trolls-are-narcissists-psychopaths-and-sadists

Krizan, Z., & Herlache, A. D. (2017). The Narcissism Spectrum Model: A Synthetic View of Narcissistic Personality. Personality and Social Psychology Review, 22(1), 3–31. https://doi.org/10.1177/1088868316685018

Mayo Clinic Staff. (2017, November 18). Narcissistic personality disorder - Symptoms and causes. Mayo Clinic. https://www.mayoclinic.org/diseases-conditions/narcissistic-personality-disorder/symptoms-causes/syc-20366662#:~:text=Although%20the%20cause%20of%20narcissistic

N. Stea Ph.D., R. Psych, J. (2020, August 21). Why Do People Troll Online? Psychology Today. https://www.psychologytoday.com/us/blog/writing-integrity/202008/why-do-people-troll-online

Ohio State News. (2014, August 5). Just One Simple Question Can Identify Narcissistic People. Just One Simple Question Can Identify Narcissistic People. https://news.osu.edu/just-one-simple-question-can-identify-narcissistic-people/

Papageorgiou, K. A., Mutz, J., Lin, Y., & Clough, P. J. (2018). Mental Toughness: A Personality Trait That Is Relevant across Achievement Contexts and Mental Health Outcomes. The SAGE Handbook of Personality and Individual Differences: Volume III: Applications of Personality and Individual, 588–603. https://doi.org/10.4135/9781526451248.n26

Psychology Today. (2019). Narcissism | Psychology Today. Psychology Today. https://www.psychologytoday.com/us/basics/narcissism

Raskin, R., & Novacek, J. (1991). Narcissism and the use of fantasy. Journal of Clinical Psychology, 47(4), 490–499. https://doi.org/10.1002/1097-4679(199107)47:4<490::aid-jclp2270470404>3.0.co;2-j

Sharma, A., Madaan, V., & Petty, F. D. (2006). Exercise for mental health. Primary Care Companion to the Journal of Clinical Psychiatry, 8(2), 106. https://doi.org/10.4088/pcc.v08n0208a

Silver, J. (2012, March 29). Is Wall Street Full of Psychopaths? The Atlantic. https://www.theatlantic.com/health/archive/2012/03/is-wall-street-full-of-psychopaths/254944/

WebMD. (2020, June 18). What are treatments for narcissistic personality disorder? WebMD. https://www.webmd.com/mental-

health/qa/what-are-treatments-for-narcissistic-
personality-disorder

What Are Personality Disorders? (2013). Psychiatry.org.
https://www.psychiatry.org/patients-
families/personality-disorders/what-are-
personality-disorders